Writers of Wales

Editors
MEIC STEPHENS   R. BRINLEY JONES

Sam Adams

THOMAS JEFFERY
LLEWELYN PRICHARD

University of Wales Press

Cardiff 2000

I

It is 1861, the year of the third major decennial census. The census enumerator for the Lower Ward of the Municipal Borough of Swansea is working his way along Thomas Street, a terrace adjacent to the saw mill, the timber yard and the gasworks. There is noise and stench from these and from the brewery in Wassail Street only a hundred yards away. Just beyond the timber yard, the criss-crossing lines of the South Dock Branch of the Great Western Railway service the busy wharfs with their bare forests of masts and spars. The census enumerator turns to schedule 201 in his sheaf of papers, approaches the junction of Thomas Street and Edward Street and knocks at the peeling door of 'Major Roteley's Cottage', a dwelling which, for all its fine-sounding address, is, if anything, humbler and more dilapidated than its neighbours. He might well sniff the air of decay and consider that this part of Swansea is indeed aptly named 'World's End'. The ragged derelict who opens the door is not extraordinary for his evident poverty (there are many like him), but he has one striking feature that is his own – yet not his own. He has a wax nose, which is more or less held in place by his spectacles. In a few words, perhaps holding a handkerchief to his own mightily assailed nostrils, the enumerator puts his official questions, and the ill-clad bundle of bones delivers up its secrets. His name is Thomas Prichard; he is the head of the household, for no one shares that dark, festering interior; he is a widower and he is 71 years old; he was born in Builth, Breconshire. Clearly he does nothing now but beg and scavenge, but what was his occupation? The old man peers at the enumerator and with what glimmer of ironic wit, what shame and regret, we cannot guess, he snuffles his response: he was formerly 'an accountant'.

Officialdom had not said its final words on the subject of Prichard, but those that remained, pronounced at the inquest into his death, were few and sad. Because there was a sudden and fortuitous revival of interest in him shortly before he died, and because of the inquest itself, more is known about the last weeks of Prichard's life than of the long and rugged road he trod in the months and years that preceded them. It seems unlikely now that any substantial testimony remains to be discovered. A cache of material had accumulated at Major Roteley's cottage in Swansea. The CAMBRIAN newspaper reported in November 1861 that the single room Prichard inhabited on the ground floor contained *a chaos of dirty and dusty books, pamphlets and MSS. in prose and poetry* among which was

a manuscript volume entitled 'Medallions of the Memorable', in a series of historic essays and sonnets [which seemed] *to display considerable literary merit as well as great historical research.*

According to one 'A. P. Thomas' writing to the 'Bye-Gones' column of the OSWESTRY ADVERTISER in December 1881, these passed into the hands of Prichard's *literary executor . . . a gentleman residing at Page Street, Swansea.* This presumably is the same *literary and patriotic gentleman of independent means then living in Glamorganshire* mentioned in the prefatory statement to the third, posthumous edition of Twm Shôn Catti published by John Pryse of Llanidloes in 1873, *who had for years been one of Mr. Prichard's best friends*, to whom *previous to his death* [he had] *made over, by a properly constructed deed all his MSS and Copyrights.* Prichard's impoverished condition when he suddenly came to the notice of the good people of Swansea shortly before his death suggests that he had been singularly short of friends. Be that as it may, there the trail ends. Pryse excuses himself from the task of writing a few details about Prichard's life by saying that he must not trespass upon the prerogative of the *benevolent gentleman* who had promised to write *a biographical account of the author's life.* No biography was published, and no Prichard manuscripts have been lodged with any of the public collections in Wales.

The scarcity of reliable information about Prichard prompts the would-be biographer to exercise imagination to fill the many gaps. It is like a particularly puzzling detective story in which the author has left too few clues to enable the reader to follow the action to the known, inevitable end. There are few primary sources: most of the documents and newspaper reports that still exist are quoted extensively in what follows and readers can draw their own conclusions from them. In the absence of further proof it is necessary to rely upon circumstantial evidence and speculation. This is no worse than the guesswork and spurious confirmation by repetition which attended attempts to set down the bare outline of his life in reference books from 1908 to 1953. T. R. Roberts (Asaph) in Eminent Welshmen puts the date of Prichard's death about 1874 and says he was born in the parish of Trallong, Breconshire. Almost five decades later the Dictionary of

NATIONAL BIOGRAPHY embellished these inaccuracies with a few of its own:

Prichard, Thomas Jeffery Llewelyn (d. 1875?), travelling actor and author; b. in the parish of Trallong, Brecknock. (He was m. at Abergavenny, 14 Jan. 1826, to Naomi Jones of Builth (SEREN GOMER, 1826, 122)). He is known to have taken part in plays given at Brecon in (e.g., 1841) and at Aberystwyth; it is also said that for some time he was employed by Lady Llanover (when she was Lady Hall) to catalogue the library in her Monmouthshire home . . . He appears to have died, in poverty, at Swansea, in 1875 (or 1876; CYFAILL YR AELWYD, 1887 (113) says he was buried there, in Tabernacle graveyard. He was alive on 24 Nov. 1875, the date of one of his letters printed in CYMRU FU, II, v, 80.)

Edwin Poole's HISTORY AND BIOGRAPHY OF BRECK-NOCKSHIRE (1886) also claims that Prichard was born in Trallong, but does not say when he was born. An examination of the parish registers of this hamlet by the side of the Usk, just off the A40, about half-way between Brecon and Sennybridge, reveals that Pritchards were fairly common there at the beginning of the nineteenth century, but not a single Thomas Prichard appears in the lists of baptisms, marriages and deaths, far less a Jeffery Llewelyn. It is clear, in any case, that the source of Poole's information was not documentary evidence which then existed in or near Brecon, but another note in 'Bye-Gones' in 1881, signed F. S. A., the original cutting of which, from the OSWESTRY ADVERTISER, is preserved in Poole's own copy of his earlier book, THE PEOPLE'S HISTORY OF BRECON, TOWN AND COUNTY (1876), at Cardiff Library:

Twm Siôn Catti (Dec. 14, 1881). T. J. Llewelyn Prichard was born in the parish of Tralloney [sic] co. Brecon, and died in

4

Swansea Union Workhouse. I cannot lay my hands upon the first three editions of the above work, but, if my memory correctly serves me, it was published by John Cox, Aberystwyth. I saw Prichard perform at the Brecon Theatre in 1841.

The date, *Dec. 14, 1881*, is that of the appearance in the same column of an enquiry about Prichard's TWM SHÔN CATTI (the spelling adopted for the 1828 edition of the book) which led to F. S. A.'s reply. While the evidence of an eye-witness that Prichard trod the boards in Brecon is acceptable, the precision of the date may be doubted; F. S. A. was casting his memory back over forty years. What of 'Tralloney'? Is it a typographical error? That seems to be admitted by the amendment to 'Trallong' that appears in the bound edition of BYE-GONES RELATING TO WALES AND THE BORDER COUNTIES (1880–1), but it could derive from a few lines of poetry by Prichard. In 'Anglesea', one of the poems in the 'Noble of Nature' sequence in WELSH MINSTRELSY, his first substantial book, Prichard pictures his *generous wand'rer* tearfully turning from *Mona, beauteous Mona* as

> *He thought of the ever-loved scenes of his childhood!*
> *Thy valleys Traloneth! thy mountain and wild-wood.*

It soon becomes clear that his steps are leading him (and here, at least, we can be sure *the Noble of Nature* is a persona adopted by the poet) to the banks of *the fair Wye* and Llanvair (*sic*), that is, *Llanvair-in-Builth*, as a note to the next poem in the sequence, 'The Sevi-Lan-Gwy', explains. 'Trallong' is occasionally anglicized to 'Trallon' in nineteenth-century documents, and may well have been pronounced 'Tralon', close enough to Prichard's 'Traloneth' to

5

suggest it was Trallong he had in mind when he penned the lines. The final syllable could have been added to obscure the Breconshire connection, or for the sake of the metre. There are, indeed, sound reasons for asserting the writer had an association with the area around Sennybridge where Trallong is located, but a number of erroneous assumptions and errors of transcription were incorporated into the reference texts: he was not born in the parish of Trallong; his wife's maiden name was James, not Jones; and the letter said to have been written in 1875 was actually dated 1857.

II

As a writer, Prichard was firstly by instinct and ambition a poet. Driven by necessity and with an eye to the main chance, he made an attempt at topographical hack-work. Fortuitously, he became a novelist, and finally an abiding interest in the heroic past of Wales and hopes of patronage led him to try his hand at history. Does he deserve to be remembered as more than a curiosity among Anglo-Welsh antecedents? The answer must be in the affirmative, if only because he was certainly among the first to consider himself Anglo-Welsh, a writer, as he put it, of *English-Welsh blossoms . . . hastily formed into a bouquet.* More than that, at its best, his poetry is comparable with that of many middle-ranking English poets of the 1820s (though it is commonly far below that standard), and he deserves recognition as the first Welsh writer to pen a novel. He is also of special interest because he held liberal beliefs and spoke out about the wretchedness of the lives of many ordinary folk in a way that allies him with some of the great minds of his time.

So far as it is now possible to tell, Prichard's first published work, a poem, 'David Gam', appeared in June 1820 in a short-lived magazine, the CAMBRO-BRITON, over the pen name 'Jeffery Llewelyn'. A second, 'Aber Edw', was printed in the September number. They were designed to catch the eye of the editor, John Humffreys Parry, who had dedicated his journal to *Wales . . . her History, her Manners, her*

Language, her Poetry, and her General Literature, in a word . . . everything Welsh, that may be deemed worthy of investigation. Parry added an editorial note to the first poem setting the historical scene – the enmity of Owain Glyndwr and Davydd Gam (the editor's preferred spelling of the names) and the latter's valour at Agincourt. As though in response, when 'Aber Edw' appeared it was with a historical and topographical note supplied by the poet. They are competent genre poems, not unlike the work of Mrs Hemans in this vein, or that of S. R. Jackson, another skilful versifier of events in Welsh history, much favoured by Parry but now totally forgotten. Both were subsequently included in WELSH MINSTRELSY, in greatly extended versions. We cannot be sure whether Parry cut the poems drastically for publication in the CAMBRO-BRITON, or Prichard, fancying quantity would please his subscribers more than quality, made hurried and lengthy additions to them for WELSH MINSTRELSY. If the latter, it was a singularly inept revision. In either case, the episode demonstrates that Prichard's self-critical faculty was poorly developed.

Evidence of unsuccessful efforts to place further poems in the CAMBRO-BRITON suggests that he had a quantity of material in manuscript and, after June 1822, when the magazine folded, nowhere to send it. If we are to believe him, he was encouraged to commit to print poems he had shown his friends. Later the same year he had MY LOWLY LOVE AND OTHER PETITE POEMS, CHIEFLY ON WELSH SUBJECTS, a 36-page pamphlet, printed at his own expense – a common enough practice – bearing on the title page his baptismal and his pen name: Thomas Jeffery Llewelyn Prichard. As we shall see, his home was at Holborn, London, but his printer, William Phillips, was in Worthing. The choice is doubly significant. Firstly, it must mean that, for a time at least, he lived in or near Worthing. Secondly, we need to ask ourselves whether it can be mere coincidence that Phillips was also the printer of that early work by Shelley (and his sister Elizabeth) ORIGINAL POETRY BY VICTOR AND CAZIRE (1810) and, more remarkably given the sensitivity of the subject, of THE NECESSITY OF ATHEISM (1811). Munday, the Oxford bookseller who had agreed to display Shelley's provocative polemic in his shop window, and within twenty minutes had an instruction from a reverend fellow of New College to burn all copies, sent a warning to Phillips of the risk of prosecution for blasphemous libel. MY LOWLY LOVE had only a thinly disguised libel of a clerical gentleman in Wales to cause the printer alarm.

Prichard prefaced his pamphlet apologetically and with a brand of pompous awkwardness that reveals him unpractised in prose:

To those of 'the friendly many and the chosen few', whose generous anxiety for my welfare, and too partial predeliction [sic] of success, have induced from year to year to repeat the often iterated question – 'Why don't you publish?' I owe some apology for my apparent niggardly manner of compliance, in the present instance . . . for putting these slight trifles into print, while, in their estimation, I have constructed and possess many a mouldering Manuscript of more solid materials, higher pretension in a poetic view, and greater amplitude. And what apology can I make? why, a simple affirmation of the fact – that I am unable to meet the expense of publishing a work of any magnitude, and the idea of printing these bagatelles was suggested by frequent requests for written Copies – (a trouble henceforth obviated) which ultimately found their way into some of the periodical works of the day, under various signatures; and thus my aim is, to prepare against marauders, and stamp the maker's name on the stragglers.

The contents include, in 'Owen Glyndower' and 'David Lloyd ap Llewelyn', pieces almost certainly written for the CAMBRO-BRITON. The former, we are told in a footnote, is from a poem called 'Howel Sele', which, though promised in later prospectuses, never saw the light of day – probably a wise decision, for 'Owen Glyndower' is a poor piece of work, as is the 'Extract from the Tale of The Lost Man (in MS.)'. Both are early evidence of Prichard's self-delusion in striving after *more solid materials, higher pretension in a poetic view, and greater amplitude.* To the contemporaries he admired, Byron certainly, Coleridge, and in all likelihood Shelley and Keats, such things were possible, but not to him. The story of how David Lloyd ap Llewelyn, a seer, took his wife's advice and prophesied Harry of Richmond's victory over Richard III is told with an agreeably light touch and is altogether more successful.

'A Lover an Ass' is in Prichard's lighter vein, and much the better for that. It is an actorly poem that begins with a little dialogue. The lover speaks:

> *Maria! – I'm an Ass! – 'an Ass!' – you cry,*
> *Yes girl, an Ass, a very Ass am I . . .*

He goes on to explain

> *An Ass is an honest, faithful, gentle slave,*
> *An ill-used subject to some jade or knave,*
> *Who stumbling, oft is on his knees;*
> *So I, thy vanity have sought to please,*
> *Blindly partial, each caprice to brave.*

> *As kneels an Indian to his wooden idol,*
> *Fool that I was! I've knelt to thee, thou sly doll.*

and concludes that, like Balaam's ass, he will turn against tyranny and *Declare thy power, and my weakness o'er*. The dramatic utterance, the deft handling of four regular rhyming stanzas, the rhyme in the final couplet above, all point to the influence of Prichard's hero, Byron.

The title poem contrasts the cynical sophistication of the town with the simplicity of the country, personified in 'my lowly love':

> *Untaught, some think her, as a fool –*
> *Some think her wild beyond all rule –*
> *But free to Nature's impulse she,*
> *And known – aye truly known to me.*

The octosyllabic rhyming couplets are more characteristic of Augustan light verse, typified by Pope's lines *Engraved in the Collar of a Dog – 'I am his Highness' dog at Kew; / Pray tell me, sir, whose dog are you?'*, but serve Prichard's purpose well enough. Soon, in the preface to WELSH MINSTRELSY, he would specifically reject the *cold, monotonous, methodical, starch English School of Poetry, that prevailed at the period sadly miscalled the Augustan age*; yet he is closer in spirit (and in some respects technically) to the Augustans than to the Romantics, largely because of the influence of Byron. The poem is of interest chiefly because of the parenthetical hint it gives of discord in his family:

> *(For I've found kindred streams of blood,*
> *To me are but a hostile flood;*

My race's name I'd fain disown,
My heart has withered in their frown.)

Two more sentimental rural poems, 'Joyce Musaderyn' and 'The Maid of Pentre Velin', which, though slight, are not without merit, also provide insights into the writer. The former has the sure imprint of first-hand knowledge of farming and the harsh realities of the countryside – an early expression of Prichard's sympathy for the labouring poor which becomes a consistent thread in his writing in verse and prose. Both name specific locations: *wild Ceven-y-mas* in 'Joyce Musaderyn' is not clearly identifiable, though there is still an old farm known as Cefn Maescar near Sennybridge, but Pentre Felin is marked little more than a mile north of Rhyd-y-briw (Sennybridge), in the first edition Ordnance Survey map of the same area (1832). Trecastle, also mentioned in the second poem, is no more than four miles to the west. This cluster of recognizable locations in Breconshire is suggestive of the poet's origins.

The booklet ends with a group of satires and squibs. Of snuff, for instance:

> *Physicians say 'tis ruinous to the brain,*
> *But such assertions are as false as vain,*
> *For those who snuffle up the useless dirt,*
> *Depend upon it – ne'er had brains to hurt.*

Others are more personal. Outstanding among these is the libellous attack on a cleric referred to above, 'A Bishop a Thief, and a Parson a Clown – addressed to the Rev. B- J- Builth':

> *If ever ruffian wore the garb of peace,*
> *Or wolf array'd him in the lamb's fair fleece –*
> *Oh such perversion, if but one there be,*
> *Thou, Reverend Ben! decidely art he.*

With its faint echo of Pope's portrait of Addison (*Who but must laugh, if such a man there be?/ Who would not weep, if Atticus were he!*), this particularly, and all the poems in the group, recall Augustan attitudes. The Bishop's part is explained in the final four lines:

> *The careless and unhallow'd mitered chief*
> *Whoever gown'd thee was – an arrant thief!*
> *Thy acts, thy manners, e'er this fact has shown*
> *He robb'd the plough-tail of a brutal clown.*

What the 'Reverend Ben' had done to Prichard, or to his family, to deserve such vitriol one can only guess at. These various clues to the writer's Breconshire connections we must, however, put aside for the moment.

'Forget Me Not', the one poem in the collection that in its subject, diction and style belongs to the 1820s, was evidently popular in its day. Prichard reprinted it in two subsequent pamphlets, on each occasion with a punning reference to *the transplanting it has met with, into Periodical Works of the day*. This, then, was the poem on which he was determined to *stamp the maker's name* lest others claim it. It is a piece of Romantic whimsy, telling how the dispute between Love, Taste and Sentiment over the naming of the flower was resolved by passing lovers:

> *While thus they talk'd, a loving pair,*
> *(A happy youth and maid;)*
> *Spent with their walk, now halted there,*

> And welcomed summer's even air,
> Beneath the willow's shade;
> And then they parted on the spot,
> Each, parting, said 'Forget me not!'

This was not Prichard's muse; 'Forget Me Not' is unlike any other of his poems.

In 1823 he had a second collection privately printed, this time in London – MARIETTE MOULINE, THE DEATH OF GLYNDOWER, AND OTHER POEMS, PARTLY ON WELSH SUBJECTS. Although it contains only fifteen poems, this is a somewhat larger pamphlet, because the poems tend to be longer and there are several pages of notes. More seriously intentioned, but not the better for that, it is again important for what it tells us about the poet rather than for the quality of the poetry. On the title page he styles himself *Author of 'My Lonely Love,' 'Theatrical Poems,' &c*, but the latter, alas, has vanished. The preface contains the same self-deprecating comments on the *petite and slight trifles* he has set before the public, and the same reason, expense, for a further failure to publish *a work of any magnitude*. But he already has a larger undertaking in mind *that will appear under the general title of 'Welsh Minstrelsy'* and will contain work compared with which the present poems are the *slightest bagatelles*. He sets out his stall for the future in a way that shows he had decided his fortune as a writer lay in his homeland:

> *Aware of the limits of their distribution, my general plan is here reversed, in the English portion of the Poems predominating over the Welsh, whereas the contrary will be the case in future: and I cannot but feel elated at the very new and flosculous field the 'Land of Cymry' represents, for rural and heroic poetry.*

14

Here too he compares himself for the first time (and protestingly) to the celebrated English rural poet Robert Bloomfield, before signing off with a pompously egotistical brio that we more readily associate with acting than writing:

. . . in spite of English prejudice against the literary efforts of Welshmen, they may ultimately be obliged to acknowledge Wales is not without her Rural Bard, *who whether or not would feel no honor* [sic] *in a comparison with their Bloomfield, the incidents of whose life have not been more inimical to the cultivation of poetry than mine . . .*

A note gives as the source of the title poem 'Kotzebue's ANECDOTES LITERARY AND PHILOSOPHICAL' from which he also derived the pathetic story of 'Alexander Claude Le Jau'. That a melodramatic mix of the sentimental and the supernatural appealed to Prichard should not surprise, for he was a creature of his age, but he was unwise to attempt to retell such tales in rhyming verse. In the process he produces some excruciating lines. Mariette stands on the parade ground awaiting the return of her faithless lover:

Whenever a gallant young officer passes,
Anxiety brightens her eye;
It catches – it fastens – hope glows and amasses –
Ah! clouded again are her blue optic glasses,
Her breast heaves a hopeless sigh.

She drowns herself. And what of the young man?

An heiress he weds of a great one in arms –
He has heard of lost Mariette, and wept for her harms;
He has wept, more than wept, the strong rending pang
Tugg'd hard at his bosom with tacit harangue . . .

and he dies in the arms of her ghost. 'The Death of Glyndower', reprinted in two later collections and, as here, with a note on the *lyric measure, peculiar to Welsh poetry*, is a poem of little sense and baffling grammar. The jaunty lyric celebrating the fruitfulness of 'Anglesea' he would use again, despite its geographical incongruity, to pad out 'The Noble of Nature' sequence in WELSH MINSTRELSY, along with 'Good Night', a love poem, and 'The Star of Liberty'. The last named, a hymn of praise to liberal beliefs, is (as we shall see later) a surprisingly overt expression of Prichard's political stance, and of a piece with his prefatorial promise to pay no regard to *the powers that be*.

In 'The Oak of Gaul' and 'The Yew of Gaul', both composed, like 'The Star of Liberty', and not entirely appositely, in octosyllabic rhyming couplets, he expresses his admiration for Napoleon and contempt for those who engineered his downfall and succeeded him. Both are sustained metaphors, explicit in their anti-government sentiment, and clear enough also in condemnation of Louis XVIII – a *much abhorr'd foul venom'd yew*, which nourishes all malignant things, *While all the liberal mind admires / Beneath its baneful shade expires*. These three poems, presumably written while Napoleon was in exile on St Helena, are Byronic in intention if not in achievement and clearly associate Prichard with the radical opposition in British politics at this time.

'The Nervous Man's Likeness', which incorporates a brief quotation from the dramatist George Colman (little remembered now but worth remarking in the context of Prichard's largely unrecorded theatrical career), is conceivably a survivor of the lost THEATRICAL POEMS, for it is a portrait of thespian moodiness convincingly from life. The opening stanzas describe the character's strange behaviour:

> *Tho' now he's so sad, and almost mad,*
> *No being at times, more gay and glad,*
> *He'll dance and sing like a woodland lad,*
> *Personified he's Hilarity:*
> *Now (pains and pleasures, each in extremes),*
> *A man possessed of devils, he seems –*
> *Yet his heart for ever bounteously teems,*
> *Towards all mankind with charity.*

Subsequently, in a different but equally well-sustained stanza form, the manic-depressive traits are displayed in dialogue with his long-suffering wife. As a light poem this is a considerable accomplishment, metrically, and in the wit of its observations.

III

There is little in the substantial bulk of WELSH MINSTRELSY (1824) to compare with the quality of especially the lighter verse in the two pamphlets discussed above. The prospectus for this book was printed in London in 1823, while Prichard was living at 25 Brook Street, Holborn. It is a lengthy and grandiose statement, first asserting that *his wayward and humble fortunes* have frustrated previous ambitions to produce a book of any substance, and secondly how much he has been encouraged to take the step by the favourable response he received to MARIETTE MOULINE. His appeal is directed not to the predominantly English readership of the pamphlet, but to the Welsh. He claims

a most decided contempt of the system of anglofying, or classification with the English, to the denial of their mother land, a habit too prevalent among my countrymen, who become fortunate in England.

His perception that the history and literature of Wales had been under-exploited by writers was reiterated in an advertisement he circulated in 1825, in which he argued

while the historical and legendary lore of England, Scotland, and Ireland have been completely ransacked, and worn threadbare in the service of the Muses, those of Wales – a land remarkable for the wildness of its legends, antiquity of its records and singular interest of its history – remain comparatively untouched; and afford a rich field for the culture of the enter-prising Poet.

The concept of a market in Welsh writing in English, and even the tone of the prospectus, he owed to the CAMBRO-BRITON and its editor John Humffreys Parry. As might have been gathered from the earlier reference to the magazine, as a source of ideas and a reference book it had a profound and inimical influence on his poetry. The standard is proclaimed at the outset by the naïve verse that appears on the title page of WELSH MINSTRELSY:

> *Heard ye the voice of the muse of the mountain?*
> *The lays of the land of the mineral fountain?*
> *Hear ye the songs of the Welsh mountaineer,*
> *The son of old Cymry – held filially dear;*
> *Oh list to the minstrel who sweeps the Welsh telyn,*
> *Hear! hear ye the harpings of* JEFFERY LLEWELYN.

The preface carries worse news. He has, he says, been persuaded by potential subscribers to change his original intentions for the book: *the 'Rural Poems,' and many of those on fictitious subjects . . . are with-drawn, to make room for such as have historical founda-tions.* This promise of unmitigated turgidity is delivered throughout the greater part of a very long book that is wholly serious in conception and only occasionally, and unintentionally, amusing.

'The Land Beneath the Sea' alone runs to 3,500 lines, without its apparatus of quoted sources and notes. Its division into three cantos suggests a writer who has fallen under the influence of the Byron of 'Don Juan', or perhaps the Keats of 'Endymion', which Prichard's poem resembles superficially in the attenuated narrative structure of a quest and in favouring, for the greater part of the text, the rhyming couplet form. In Keats's poem, the shepherd-prince Endymion, searching for Cynthia, the moon, descends into the depths of the earth to find her, and the legends of Venus and Adonis, Glaucus and Scylla, and Arethusa are quite deftly woven into the story. Prichard clumsily incorporates the familiar narrative of Cantref y Gwaelod into the stories of a blind old man, a woman in grey, and Celin, a youthful harpist, also blind, whose name conveniently rhymes with *telyn*, and is revealed in the last few lines as the old man's son. Occasional passages allow the reader some short-lived relief of tedium. Blind Celin gives his perception of a sultry haze in an extended image that would not have entirely disgraced Coleridge:

> 'Ha, ha!' laughed he, 'now who but me
> Can see the hands that weave the haze?
> Their shuttle, a star, flies to and fro,
> Like a shooting meteor's glow,
> That merry spirits from east to west,
> As children their toys in joys and fest
> To one another throw:
> 'Ha, ha!' laughed he, 'now who but me,
> Can see the texture grow?'

A little later, in the midst of this atmospheric disturbance, a character at a local inn tells of the curative influence of Celin's music on 'Old Goody Evans of Trecastle', who, twenty years before Edgar Allan Poe penned his famous poem, had a very similar experience with a raven:

> He [sic] said, 'I'll never get to heaven!
> For on my bed-post, lo! a raven,

Still perches every day,
And there he croaks – be kind good folks,
Oh drive the fiend away!'

Passages of confident versification, when the narrative bowls along, are few and, like blind Celin's vision of the turbulent sky, may be accompanied by Coleridgean echoes. *Oh she was fair as fair could be! /* *Her skin was like transparency* . . . evokes 'The Ancient Mariner', while Celin's mother's tale, in which *the mastiff barked* and there is a powerful, if uncertain, sexual threat, recalls 'Christabel':

I know not what could make me scream,
For it was HE, that pleasured me,
The youth I saw in my dream:
He caught me – fainting – in his arms,
Pray Heaven he did me no further harms.

Topographical description, especially of St David's, where the story ends, suggests first-hand observation in addition to the use of sources like Fenton's PEMBROKESHIRE, quoted in the notes. Parts of the poem may well have been written in some haste, after Prichard's return to Wales and probably while he was soliciting subscriptions for his book: the text contains many typographical errors and solecisms. We are told that, while he was staying at Aberystwyth in 1839, Tennyson read 'The Land Beneath the Sea' and was moved to laughter by it. Any reader who attempts it today will not for one moment wonder why.

The preface to 'The Noble of Nature' explains that it has been substituted for 'Howel Sele' (*a part of that Manuscript having been unluckily mislaid, its publication at present is unavoidably delayed*) and acknowledges that the sequence is *but a thin adumbration of character, to connect a parcel of smaller Poems together –* a few of which had appeared in the two earlier pamphlets. Although bearing the marks of haste in composition, or sheer carelessness, this is a more interesting work.

The character of *the Noble of Nature* emerges as a conflation of the Byronic hero, a personification of liberal ideals, and Prichard himself. An introductory sonnet conveys a good deal about Prichard's perception of the circumstances that have held him back. 'Necessity' and 'Poverty' have reduced the brave and free to slavery, sucked away energy, and *stamped misanthropy on friendship's face*. The title poem of the sequence continues the theme of worthiness rejected:

> *The Noble of Nature was lowly of birth,*
> *Integrity's fav'rite! with true soul of worth.*
> *The Arts and the Sciences smiled on his youth,*
> *And his was humility, wisdom, and truth;*
> *But the Noble of Nature was born to endure,*
> *And stood in his nation a stranger, and poor.*

'My Chosen', next in the sequence, is a love poem to one beautiful and *unassuming,* whose face *all intelligence pourtrays* [sic]. He pledges himself to cherish her – *Yet no . . . she / Who'd be a Heaven on earth to me, / I would not lead to poverty*. Through the excess verbiage, especially in 'My Chosen', which is a victim of the writer's tendency to enlarge to absurdity, a sense of injustice emerges to add to that theme of the unnatural rejection of claims of kinship identified earlier. Even were there no supporting evidence, the reader might well conclude that Prichard saw himself a returning exile, robbed of his birthright and exceedingly hard done by.

The poem 'My Lowly Love', reprinted here, is also the worse for enlargement, but some of its sentimental charm remains. The conventional pastoral praise for a simple rural maid throws into sharp relief the rather remarkable poem that follows. 'The Woes of the Cottage' deals with the harsh reality of life in *highland or valley of Wales* where *Scenes of Arcadia, in poesy fair* are *Supplanted by poverty, labour, and care*. What follows is an antidote to the Romantic view of nature, from Wordsworth to Samuel Palmer:

> *When Winter is raging with fearfullest ire,*
> *The furze of the mountainside, uprooted for fire,*
> *The cottager gathers, which burns quick as straw,*
> *The earth-floor's a mud-pool, all drenched with a thaw!*
> *Cold drops from the thatch over table and bed,*
> *The soul-piercing draughts, smiting Happiness dead!*
> *Half-clad trembling urchins growl o'er their scant pottage; –*
> *Keen, keen are the woes, oh the woes of the cottage.*

And while, in spite of all, virtue persists in some of the peasantry, we are not allowed the satisfaction of supposing that this miserable existence breeds stoicism and honesty: *The cottage has vices, base vices as well.*

> *Ah! who then can covet the poor peasant's lot?*
> *Turmoil and misery await on the cot;*
> *Sickness and beggary – his rent in arrear –*
> *Driven forth by hard landlord in season severe!*
> *A heart-broken outcast that sufferings decay,*
> *A mere beast of burthen forth hunted away!*
> *His parish-bred young ones – Calamity's hot rage –*
> *Keen, keen, are the woes, the dread woes of the cottage.*

The naïvety of the versification does not entirely dissipate the strength of these lines. As criticism of society's neglect of the rural poor, there is little in the main-stream of English poetry to match them until Thomas Hood published 'The Lay of the Labourer' in 1844.

The additional lines that link the reprinted 'Angle-sea' to the next poem in the sequence, 'The Sevi-Lan-Gwy', contain those references to 'Traloneth' and 'Llanvair' mentioned earlier, which suggest that the author's origins lay in the Builth Wells area and that he had a connection with Trallong. A note claims that the 'sevi' or, in English, 'sive' (more properly cive or chive) grows wild only on the banks of the Wye, and that it is the true emblem of Wales, not the leek. *The finest I ever saw*, Prichard continues, *grew on a small isolated rock in the middle of the Wye, near Builth*. The poetic version of the tale is tediously longer, and far clumsier, than the prose, but occasional lines catch the eye. The Welsh prince who *consecrated* [the sevi] *first to brave Honour* is eulogized as its *high liberal donor*; and the English are the *sons of the sais* who, with their *vulture king* and *thrice num'rous host*, have usurped the domain of Liberty. With the loss of freedom, the nation's songs and treasured archives have disappeared, its mansions have decayed and its language has declined. The *innocent, cheerful, eve's dance on the green* has been replaced by

> *. . . a barbarous scene*
> *Of jumping fanatics, whose dolorous yell*
> *Remind of the fabled vile orgies of hell;*
> *The frantic enthusiast's rant is preferred*
> *To the minstrel's sweet song once gratefully heard.*

If the chronology is wayward, at least the critique of nonconformist fanaticism is clear. This is the revenge of Prichard the actor.

An epigraph from Byron introduces 'The Legend of Aberedw', and from the opening, *Know ye the spot where the Sevi of Cambria / Withers in woe for her children's misdeeds?*, with its clear echo of, *Know ye the land where the cypress and myrtle / Are emblems of deeds that are done in their clime?*, from 'The Bride of Abydos', it strives to be Byronic in mood and versification.

The betrayal of Llywelyn ap Gruffudd is dealt with summarily in the second stanza; much of the rest describes how the curse of the prince's bard has reduced a fair town to a *village of cots*. Frequently flawed though it is, 'The Legend of Aberedw' is the most carefully crafted poem in WELSH MINSTRELSY. In marked contrast, 'Llewenny', which follows it, has some extraordinary lines:

> *Here too, on the banks of Llewenny,*
> *The florid farm-girls of the vales*
> *Sing the loud song, while milking at eve,*
> *Or morn, scouring milking pails.*

'The Maid of Pentre Velin', reprinted here from MY LOWLY LOVE, and 'The Mountain Ash of Llwyn-y-neath' are chiefly remarkable (notwithstanding the unusually well-sustained verse pattern of the latter) for the identifiable locations mentioned earlier. The farm named Llwyn-nyth appears on the 1832 OS map north of Rhyd-y-briw and about a mile to the west of the hamlet of Pentre-felin.

As we have seen, in his preface to MARIETTE MOULINE, Prichard compared himself to Robert Bloomfield. There he claimed that the latter's life had not been *more inimical to the cultivation of poetry* than his own, some of the particulars of which he said he had *related in the Preface to my unpublished Poem called 'The Land Beneath the Sea'*. These biographical notes did not, however, find a place in WELSH MINSTRELSY and we are left with only hints of great expectations frustrated. Their absence may also indicate that he suppressed overt criticism of wealthy relatives while the hope of benefaction from them lingered.

'The Star of Liberty' has an epigraph from Coleridge and the whole of poem is imbued with the Pantisocratic vision of the Cambridge undergraduate who, in the summer of 1794, had made a walking tour through Wales, following the Wye at first, before pressing north, via Llanfyllin and Bala, to Beaumaris. Prichard, aged four, in his Wye valley home, might have seen Coleridge tramp by and wondered at the grotesquely decorated five-foot walking stick the stranger carried. As a young man of liberal views he would certainly have read in THE FRIEND in 1809 Coleridge's account of the utopian plan that took shape in his mind during the walking tour – *a plan as harmless as it was extravagant, of trying the experiment of human Perfectibility on the banks of the Susquahannah.* The first line of 'The Star of Liberty', *Oh! that I were an Indian wild* places Prichard's utopia, like that of his inspirer, in North America. What does perfect liberty signify to Prichard? It means free love with a *tawny maid*, a beneficent nature (*The sea, the woods, should render food*) and freedom from the oppressive regimes of the *nations miscalled civilized*. Coleridge's *undivided Dale of Industry* is reflected in *No heartless master's eye should awe, / And impose the despot law . . . no wasting toil for niggard pay.* Significantly, in the context of the writer's personal troubles, among those excluded

from this land of plenty and justice for all are the
bloated priest and the *scoundrel lawyer*. The poem ends
with a formidable peroration:

> *Oh! that I were and* [sic] *Indian free!*
> *The savage son of Liberty!*
> *Far from Europe's sons of blood,*
> *The homicidal viper brood!*
> *Where men are as utensils made,*
> *Mere tools of art; where war's a trade –*
> *Religion craft; where best is he*
> *Who stabs the heart of Liberty.*

News of Byron's death at Missolonghi in April 1824
would have reached Prichard while he was in the
later stages of gathering subscribers for WELSH
MINSTRELSY. It gave a final Byronic bias to 'The Noble
of Nature', which ends with an extravagant elegy:

> *The princely nobleman, the gifted bard,*
> *The true philanthropist, the friend of man,*
> *Oh he that Freedom held in dear regard,*
> *Prepared to perish, foremost in the van,*
> *To rescue Greece from vassalage! ill starred*
> *Who, who, shall deem him that the great course ran?*
> *He sleeps in the land of his loveliest lays,*
> *The greatest, brightest, noblest of his days.*

The last sixty or so pages of the book are occupied by a
baker's dozen of historical poems, all designed to
praise the Welsh, and most to denigrate the English –
the treacherous English, the half-converted, heathen-hearted
Saxons. A note quotes Pennant on *the long prejudice of*
the English against the Welsh. Celebration of the Tudor
dynasty provides an opportunity to draw a contrast
between the way in which the pride of *long-crushed*
Cambria is at last restored not by a *gory rout* in the

English style, but by the love of Owen Tudor and Henry V's widow Catherine. Although they have many weaknesses, some polish has been applied to these poems. They, above all, are what the prospectus to WELSH MINSTRELSY promised. With the prospectus and the preface to the book, they represent the high-water mark of Prichard's enthusiasm for Wales and the Welsh language.

IV

While WELSH MINSTRELSY was in the press, Prichard busied himself with two projects, a piece of historical and topographical hack-work in prose, THE NEW ABERYSTWYTH GUIDE, and, to accompany it, a third pamphlet, ABERYSTWYTH IN MINIATURE, IN VARIOUS POEMS. The preface to the latter introduces that notion of 'English-Welsh' writing mentioned earlier, and promises those that find in it *the Sweet-briar, or the Nettle* that he intended *more of good than harm – of mirth than mischief.* Five of the sixteen poems had appeared in one or other of the earlier pamphlets, and 'The Forget Me Not' in both. 'Welsh Food', a light-hearted eulogy of *sweet new milk and flummery*, he would use again in TWM SHÔN CATTI. 'A Bishop a Thief, and a Parson a Clown' is given a new title, 'The Robbery – sketched from an original at Builth, Brecknockshire', and accompanied by an 'Epigram' on the same subject:

> *Our reverend Pastor, some aver,*
> *Misleads the flock beneath his care,*
> *Nor boasts he skill to rear them;*
> *Every branch of Shepherd art*
> *Perchance he hath not quite by heart,*
> *But, truth to say, none more expert*
> *Than Parson B– to shear them.*

Most of the new poems make what they can of the history and picturesque scenery of Aberystwyth – 'The Walks of the Castle Ruins', 'Pendinas' and the lamentable 'Plas Creeg' among them. Anger was Prichard's finest inspiration, not history, and where there are caustic comments to be made, for example about private and civic neglect of the town's chalybeate 'Mineral Spring', the language is usually crisp and the versification sure. Such is his disgust at the dire conditions of the inhabitants of 'The Cottage, One of the Many near Aberystwyth', which, as a note explains, *line one side of the road from Trevechan to the first Turnpike-gate on the Cardigan Road*, that the language can barely contain the violence of his feelings. It says a great deal for Prichard's moral, and perhaps physical, courage that he would speak out against the neglectful landlords of these desperate tenants (as he may have done later when faced by a powerful and arrogant patron with whose views he disagreed). The poem re-emphasizes the theme of 'The Woes of the Cottage':

Is this a human habitation? – this!
Gracious and eternal powers! yes –
Men, women, children, litter in this stye,
And poorly shelter'd from the Seasons lie . . .

Poor heart-struck victims of the season's ire:
Thus nerveless, squalid, hopeless, and inert,
In sullen vassalage to care and dirt . . .

And this the kingdom too, that nations prize!
So prompt to doctrinate and civilize
The land of Savages, and infidels,
Where human degradation never swells
To such a sordid and debased extreme. –
Quixotic missionaries! no more dream
Of foreign conversion feats – but cease to roam,
Convert the WEALTHY HEATHENS here at home . . .

The poem has a declamatory style that would remind us of Prichard's other calling even if the pamphlet had not included a remarkable opening poem largely concerned with the status of the theatre in the town – 'The Drama's Petition to the Ladies and Gentlemen of Aberystwith' (*sic*). This is primarily a plea that plays and players should be better housed, and it reveals Prichard's close knowledge of the stage. We gather that, in 1824, Aberystwyth had two acting venues and a regular touring company, all of which 'Drama' condemns:

> *. . . oh! from Bridge-Street set me, set me free!*
> *Where boors annoy me with their clownish laughters,*
> *When strikes my head against the beams and rafters*
>
> . . .
>
> *Rid me from cobwebs and from Penglaise* [sic] *barn,*
> *Rid me of players who resemble ganders,*
> *More vain than peacocks, and too dull to learn,*
> *Rid me of Saunders* [sic]*, and the crew of Saunders . . .*

Whether this criticism had a bearing on the matter or not it is impossible to say, but the troupe led by the comedian Charles Sanders, which had provided theatrical entertainments at Aberystwyth each summer season since 1816, did not return after 1824. The *frightful hole / In gloomy Bridge-Street* probably continued in use until 1833 when a new playhouse opened. The poem responds to the complaint of *sullen Bigotry* and *gaping Fanaticism* that the theatre encouraged vice and eulogizes it as the *mansion of rational pleasure* of *Moral, / Polish'd diction, and Elegance . . . Mirth and Innocence. British Shakespeare* is celebrated as *my English tutor*, and Ben Jonson as a *wise seer*, while the *mystifyers* of German drama and the *cap'ring* French are dismissed, and Dryden and Wycherly castigated as representatives of the *base licentiousness* [that] *then pleased the times*. The dramatists Prichard mentions who are closer to his own time are of particular interest – *Farquhar, Sheridan, and the Colmans twain* [and] . . . *Moreton* – as names that occur frequently in playbills of the period.

'Drama's Petition' offers more than a defence and genealogy of theatre. As the prose gloss that precedes the poem indicates, it *expatiates on certain Cardiganshire cottages*, that is, it returns to the attack on landowners who house the poor peasantry in hovels *ten times viler than a dog house*, and warns – *If brutal dwellings to the poor ye suit, / What wonder if man degenerates to brute?* These are contrasted with the wise landowners who treat their tenants with humanity – the Earl of Lisburne, and W. Lewis Esq. of Llaniron (both of whom, we see from the subscribers' list, took three copies of WELSH MINSTRELSY). The case of a Captain Lewis, a local entrepreneur, is handled with delightful irony. His visionary projects included building a coastal turnpike road, and houses from stone dislodged by quarry blasting, but (as a note to the poem points out) the rate of construction, *about one house per year*, does not encourage hope of realization of the grand plans. It is with tongue in cheek that 'Drama' pleads, *Gentlemen! listen to the boon I ask, / Let Captain Lewis build a house for me.*

The poem begins with an epigraph from Byron and it is composed, fluently in the main, in *ottava rima*, the 'Don Juan' stanza form, with a sprinkling of suitably Byronic rhymes. Typically uneven, it is still among Prichard's finest achievements in poetry, if not quite the best:

> *At present I occupy a frightful hole*
> *In gloomy Bridge-Street, on the banks of Rheidol,*

> *I, too! a lady of a lofty soul,*
> *Fashion's darling, and Improvement's idol!*
> *I – who the vices of the age controul,*
> *And pay to virtue, let me say, a high toll,*
> *For one of my poets well assigns my part,*
> *'To raise the genius, and to mend the heart.'*

Even here, however, he cannot resist interpolating into the midst a dreadful *elegy, in alliteration* re-telling the story of Cantref y Gwaelod.

Prichard's novel, TWM SHÔN CATTI, is (as the full title has it) 'interspersed with poems'. The first is 'Milk and Flummery', reprinted without change from ABERYSTWYTH IN MINIATURE, where it was entitled 'Welsh Food'. The second is a jolly bidder's song, which is accompanied by a note on biddings, almost verbatim, from the CAMBRO-BRITON, where the poem would have been published had the magazine not suddenly ceased publication in June 1822. Somewhat later, Twm, disguised as a woman, sings ballads at Cardigan fair. Two of these are borrowed, with acknowledgement, from other sources – as are a few briefer verses scattered elsewhere in the book – but the third, untitled, ballad is Prichard's own, and particularly significant. In these unsophisticated stanzas the writer is surely referring not to his hero Twm's, but to his own childhood and the places he knew as a child:

> *When a wild rural Welsh boy I ran o'er the hills,*
> *And sprang o'er the hedges, the gates, brooks and rills,*
> *The high oak I climb'd for the nest of the kite,*
> *And plung'd in the river with lively delight!*
> *Ah who then so cheerful, so happy as me,*
> *As I skipp'd through the woodlands and meads of Brindee.*

'Brindee' is clearly Bryn-du. There may be a multitude of locations in Wales bearing that name, but this Bryn-du is pinpointed by further references in the poem to 'Llwyn-y-neath' (Llwyn-nyth – already identified near Rhyd-y-briw on the 1832 OS map of Brecknockshire), and 'Dyvonnock' (Defynnog, barely a mile south of Rhyd-y-briw). It is another farm, isolated, high on the hillside overlooking the A40 and the mountains to the south, about a mile to the north-east of Llwyn-nyth. Like the bidder's song, this was probably a poem Prichard had retained unpublished from his London days, when, with an ambition to emulate Bloomfield's rural muse, he could write as an exile, *Oh bless'd were those days! long departed from me, / Far, far's my loved Cambria! far far is Brindee.*

Little else remains of Prichard's output in poetry: five of his own historical pieces (including a ballad of excruciating clumsiness and naïvety entitled 'The Worthies of Wales'), which appear alongside the more polished work of Mrs Hemans, S. R. Jackson and others in THE CAMBRIAN WREATH, an anthology for the tourist market that he had printed and bound in some style in Aberystwyth in 1828; lines from a 'Comic Poem . . . called Davydd ab Gwilym' quoted (as we shall see) in the LLANDRINDOD GUIDE; and a few poems contributed to 'Poets' Corner' in the CAMBRIAN newspaper from an address at High Street, Swansea in August 1824, two of which he had published previously. That a good deal more remained in manuscript, and passed into the hands of the *gentleman residing in Page Street, Swansea* on his death, there is no reason to doubt, but they did not find their way into print and, we must conclude, have been destroyed. If they resembled the work that he set most store by, the loss has been trifling. If, on the other hand, they had a satirical edge, if they were occasionally humorous in their observation of character, and if, from time to time, inspired by anger, we may have lost as trenchant a poetic commentary on Wales in the first half of the nineteenth century as ever John Tripp and Harri Webb supplied on the second half of the twentieth.

V

A flavour of Prichard's prose has already been conveyed in the quoted extracts from various prefaces. He was a little ponderous, not to say pompous, on these occasions, by turns defensive and over-assertive about his claims as a poet. More generally, he has a fluent, if mannered, style that adapts well enough to light, humorous fiction and satire, and can catch fire when he is angered by his subject.

His first prose book was THE NEW ABERYSTWYTH GUIDE TO THE WATERS, BATHING HOUSES, PUBLIC WALKS etc., published in 1824. Inevitably, it offers yet another account of *the Lowland Hundred inundated by the Sea* along with material also used in WELSH MINSTRELSY concerning *the exploits of Owen Glyndower*, and topographical and other information from a variety of acknowledged sources. It seems to have been commissioned by a local bookseller, Lewis Jones, and is of far less interest than the pamphlet of poems, ABERYSTWITH IN MINIATURE, that accompanied it. However, the ease with which it was brought off inspired a grand project – the CAMBRIAN BALNEA: OR GUIDE TO THE WATERING PLACES OF WALES, MARINE AND INLAND, which was conceived as a periodical publication to be completed in ten numbers. In the prospectus, dated 1825, he claimed the motive for the work was

A passionate desire to rescue from unmerited obscurity

whatever relates to Wales, and remove, as far as my limited ability permits, the stigma too justly cast on modern Welshmen for an unaccountable apathy in what regards their local pre-eminence, or national improvement . . .

In addition to historical and topographical descriptions, analyses of the mineral spas and doctors' opinions on the medical conditions they alleviated, the BALNEA promised *Incidental Anecdotes connected with the History and Antiquities of this Interesting Principality* – the mixture much as in the ABERYSTWYTH GUIDE, and intended for the English tourist in Wales.

The prospectus referred to the BALNEA as being *in the press*, for he had already completed early in 1825 what he would now term a 'part' of it, the LLANDRINDOD GUIDE. The speed of production was due in large measure to Prichard's familiarity with that area and to the availability of a new edition of the ANALYSIS OF THE MEDICINAL WATERS OF LLANDRINDOD etc. by Richard Williams, which had been advertised in the CAMBRO-BRITON in July 1820. He had the permission of Williams, resident surgeon at Aberystwyth, for extensive borrowings. Much the most interesting passage in the guide is a lengthy and vicious digression on a landowner, Edward Burton, whose memorial tablet is an insignificant feature of the church at Llandewi Ystradenny:

[Burton] *resided here, very penuriously, in a large old house, and possessed a considerable estate in the neighbourhood, which, to the exclusion of his relatives, because they were poor, he basely devised to a wealthy provincial! If there is a scoundrel baseness, a mental degradation marking the most decided abjectness of soul, surpassing all others in its abuses of the social compact, it is an heartless, cold-blooded act like this, which often leaves to waste, in corrosive rust, the brightest link in the chain of consanguinity – the poor helpless one, the lost sheep of the fold . . .*

If there were any doubt how closely Prichard's own case resembled that of Burton's poor relatives, the quotation that follows from the *unpublished Comic Poem . . . called Davydd ab Gwilym* dispels it:

> *Here I think it needful to observe,*
> *And I remark it with a wincing grin,*
> *As well such sore place truly may deserve,*
> *The strangeness of relatives to their kin,*
> *Whose narrow fortunes bid them leanly carve, –*
> *Poverty alone their deadly sin:*
> *(Not that mine have left me so to starve,*
> *For I have independence – that's* within:*)*
> *To those in affluence, high state, and station,*
> *Pride, or shame, whichever it may be,*
> *Will prompt them, sometimes to be wondrous civil;*
> *To send them to a distance off – to sea –*
> *Could wishes do it, even to the devil;*
> *Out of the world at any rate: for me,*
> *I can't swear mine are quite so sunk in evil.*
> *The rich and heartless one, but* power *lacks*
> *To shoot such scrubs, as Planters do the blacks.*

An advertisement on the last page of the LLAN-DRINDOD GUIDE promised a great deal in subsequent numbers of the CAMBRIAN BALNEA, including, among *several select biographical notices* one of *the notorious Twm Siôn Catti . . . with a detail of his knavish exploits, partly translated from the Welsh and now first collected.* No further number appeared, but around the material Prichard had collected about Twm Siôn Catti grew an accretion of traditional story, invention, quasi-historical embroidery and contemporary social comment that, when it was eventually published, made it (in the eyes of some) the first Welsh novel.

THE ADVENTURES AND VAGARIES OF TWM SHÔN CATTI was published in Aberystwyth in 1828. This first edition was a cheap affair, clumsily printed on coarse paper, which was all that Prichard could afford. It was not seen through the press with any care: there are two chapters numbered VII, a further two numbered XXI, and XVIII is missing, so that, although there are twenty-eight chapters in all, the last is numbered XXVII. How the anonymous reviewer in the CAMBRIAN QUARTERLY (Vol. 1, 1829) could praise its *printing, matter and materials* is a mystery. The subsequent criticism of the book by Idrison (William Owen Pughe) in the same journal (Vol. 2, 1830) for its historical inaccuracy makes as little sense. It is a late example of the eighteenth-century picaresque narrative, as exemplified especially by Fielding, but unstructured, a rag-bag, 'descriptive of life in Wales: interspersed with poems', as the full title goes on to say, to which the ramshackle framework of Twm's legendary adventures provides some sort of unity. The author, who is satirical and amusing, frequently stalls the progress of events to comment – on the ignorance of Welsh history and legend among the English; on the condescending attitude of English gentleman-farmers who *civilize* the Welsh by appropriating their land; on Methodism's *puritanic gloom*; on *flummery and milk*, and so on. The social comment can be bitterly ironic:

Alas for the good old days . . . Days approved of by the great, and therefore good; when the humbler sons of industry looked up to them as gods, and they returned the compliment by looking down on their worshippers as good and well-taught dogs, that earned their bones and scraps . . . Days when . . . a sycophantic subserviency paved the way to wealth and honours – when the gross vice of manly independence was unknown, and no class acknowledged among men, but the high and the low, or the rich and the poor.

The English generally, and English landowners in particular, feel Prichard's lash:

the half-bred English gentlemen who literally infest Wales, and become nuisances and living grievances to the people – building their pretensions to superiority and fashion, on a sneering self-sufficiency, and scorn of customs and peculiarities merely because they are Welsh.

At the outset, Squire Graspacre is much like these; he personifies the cheating, rapacious incomer who robs the *poor little freeholders* of their few acres. But Prichard is not constrained by any notions of consistency in the portrayal of character. By chapter VII the grasping squire has undergone a personality change so that he can also represent that rare breed, the liberal landowner, sufficiently interested in Welsh customs to employ servants from *all the different counties of South Wales*, and dress them in their local costumes.

The 'plot' is episodic and subservient to Prichard's aims to satirize the English, defend Welsh culture and display folk customs. It includes several historical figures, but with scant regard for the facts of their lives and none for chronology. Catti (Catherine) lives, in straitened circumstances, as a tenant at Llidiard-y-Fynnon [*sic*], what remains of the Tregaron farm her family once possessed, now owned by Graspacre. Sir John Wynn of Gwydir, brother-in-law of the squire, while visiting Graspacre Hall chances to see Catti and wonders whether she is *come-at-able*. She is – and the outcome is Twm, who, since he has no regular father, is known as the son of 'Shôn' and Catti. Sir John buys Llidiard-y-Fynnon from Graspacre and gives it to Catti, who sets up a happy, if illiterate, school on the premises. Catti is made to court Jack o Sîr Gâr, a successful wooden spoon and clog-sole manufacturer, and vast trencherman of hideous aspect, in order to introduce the diversions of milk and flummery and 'bundling' and, in due course, the 'bidding' and a Welsh wedding.

Graspacre, suddenly a widower, establishes John David Rhys, a young man of high intelligence and impeccable Welshness (and a historical figure transplanted), as the local curate and tutor to Twm. Then, in another *volte face*, he declares Twm over-educated for his station in life and orders him to be dismissed from school. Twm is sent as apprentice to the farmer Morris Grump, as his name implies, a morose character. This episode seems chiefly designed to allow Prichard to include some romantic descriptions of upland Cardiganshire. The Grump family is wiped out by smallpox and Twm returns to Tregaron to enter the service of Graspacre. Under Rhys's direction the boy grows to love books, though not those of a religious tendency, but this has the effect (much as we must believe it had in the case of the writer himself) of making him aware of his poverty and discontented with his lot in life. Twm falls for Gwenny Cadwgan and saves her from the evil designs of Graspacre, who, in yet another change, has acquired vices. Graspacre's children return home to illustrate some of the worst characteristics of English ignorance and boorishness. Young Twm, on the other hand, has *rare qualities of good nature and cheerfulness* together with *satirical and mischievous propensities*. He falls foul of Marmaduke, Graspacre's son and heir, thrashes him and escapes, finding refuge with Rhys the curate. Rhys's admonishment, *while you live, whatever your state while on earth, act the generous and manly part; and never, never, either manually or with the lash of satire, war with the weak*, reinforces the notion that Twm is, in part, an idealized self-portrait of Prichard. A marriage is arranged with Gwenny Cadwgan, but before it can be solemnized another violent encounter with Marmaduke results in Twm taking flight from his *dear native town, which a fashionable tourist would perhaps have called the most wretched village in the universe*. Using disguise and mimicry, he eludes would-be captors and escapes. He has unpremeditatedly become a thief, and is in turn robbed by others when he seeks to make restitution.

At this point the adventures come thick and fast. Twm, disguised as a woman, sings ballads at Cardigan fair; discovered there, he again uses cunning to escape. He meets Rhys, who has also left Tregaron, at Lampeter and hears from him a 'tragical tale'. An account of their trek over the desolate moorland towards Llandovery provides Prichard with an opportunity to describe the scenery and the abject poverty of the peasants there. Twm rescues the heiress of Ystrad Fîn (*sic*) from a highwayman and is handsomely rewarded by Sir George Devereux, the lady's husband, on their arrival at Llandovery. Subsequently, Sir George entrusts to him the carriage of a sum of money to London. Again he encounters a highwayman and, not without difficulty, outwits him. He learns from a pig drover that his love Gwenny has died in childbirth in Tregaron. His remorse is moderated by the feelings he now has for the Lady of Ystrad Fîn. En route once more, he overcomes another highwayman, and then a footpad, whom he shoots dead. He returns to Wales to find that Sir George Devereux has conveniently died in a fall from an ill-broken horse: he pursues the widow – successfully, but they are parted by gossiping scandalmongers. He has a series of rural adventures, which bear all the characteristics of folk-tale, in every case winning through by trickery and wit. He makes a temporary home in a cave, which the author, having visited it, describes in detail. Returned to Brecon, he is successful at the eisteddfod, at the races and a ball, and at last marries the grand lady.

The ABERYSTWYTH GUIDE and the CAMBRIAN BALNEA/ LLANDRINDOD GUIDE were principally intended for English visitors to Wales, but TWM SHÔN CATTI was written for a Welsh readership, perhaps in consequence of the failure of the BALNEA. Prichard's view, expressed early in the book, that *neither legends, poetry, nor history of the principality, serves to interest or accord with the queasy taste of our English bretheren*, is a measure of his disenchantment with the tourist market. As an unpretentious, lively entertainment, the first edition was a popular success, and still has a great deal to offer.

In the preface to the second edition he records how the reception of the book by the public in Wales had been *infinitely beyond the author's expectation*, due, in part, to the suggestion that *slight as it was, it was the first attempted thing that could bear the title of a Welsh novel.* He set about rewriting it in the 1830s with the clear intention of making a novel that could compete for English trade. Comments in the text suggest that Prichard, probably inspired by Dickens's success, had attempted to interest an English publisher:

However partial some amiable prosers may be to long stories, as evinced by those gentle writers, who have the orthodox number of three volumes to make up, before a fashionable publisher will treat with them, we confess our absolute aversion to them. And in this humble provincial tale, our constant aim has been to condense . . . [and later] *. . . we are not engaged by any great metropolitan publisher to beat out our little morsel of gold into the extensive surface of three half-guinea volumes . . .*

This rejection of the metropolitan market, and insistence on unmodish brevity, might be more convincing if it did not occur where Prichard was considerably expanding the original. That much of the work was done not long before publication is clear from the book's indebtedness to THE PICKWICK PAPERS (1836–7) and OLIVER TWIST (1838). It is not difficult to recognize Dickensian elements. Sir George Devereux, now *the sporting baronet* (a greatly extended portrait), is given the oral characteristics of Mr Jingle:

. . . balance against us – owe thee much – Joan's life – thy merry company, but how the devil to part with thee; joy to thee, this London – death to me – no fox-hunting, all smoke and devilment . . .

while an entirely new character, Moses, *the deserted bantling of a rascally Jew, who deceived the silly wench of a hedge-ale-house maid*, like the starving boys in OLIVER TWIST, has fantasies of eating.

44

Twm Shôn Catty (the spelling adopted for the 1839 edition) is far more sophisticated structurally than the first attempt, and far longer, but the additions of character and incident are almost without exception derivative, as well as coarsened, and the text is often stylistically turgid. Even then Prichard had not finished with his *humble provincial tale*: among the manuscripts and copyrights he sold to that *literary and patriotic gentleman of independent means*, was the revised and further extended version printed by John Pryse of Llanidloes in 1873. This text was edited for the press with some care. Solecisms that had lingered into the second edition were corrected, and the eccentric numbering of chapters was at last banished. The amateurishness, and much of the charm, of Prichard's first inspiration was no more.

It is reasonable to suppose that a good deal of the writer's time during the 1840s was spent on researching and writing his last book, Heroines of Welsh History, published in 1854. Though long, and grandiloquent in tone, it is an interesting collection of ancient, and some more recent, historical and quasi-historical material. Notwithstanding the name of a 'heroine' at each chapter head, it is at least as much concerned with heroes, and essentially, a clumsy, because alphabetically organized, history of Wales. It owes a good deal to The Cambrian Plutarch (1824), John Humffreys Parry's chronologically organized collection of *biographical notices of the more eminent natives of the Principality*. Prichard (who, as we shall see, had other debts to Parry) may have had second thoughts about his scheme. In a note to the chapter on 'Bella the Fortune-teller' he helpfully (not to say patronizingly) points out that *by a reference to the different epochs in which these characters flourished, the book can be read according to the order of chronology. Thus the candid examiner . . . may find the attempt to render it a* Biographical History of the Principality of Wales, *not altogether a failure, even at his first attempt at such an arduous undertaking.*

The book is chiefly interesting now for what it tells us in notes and asides about the development of Prichard's views on Wales and the Welsh language. That 'Eleanor de Montford' and 'Catherine of France' should find a place in the book is no surprise, but why Dolly Pentraeth, the last Cornish speaker? It is clearly to give expression to the following:

To the utilitarian, whose creed and mental aspirations favour nothing but progress, [the death of a language] . . . is 'a consumation devoutly to be wished'; but to the philosopher, or profound meditator on the death of nations and the general mutability of human affairs, not the less interesting, or intensely affecting – however . . . ardently [he may] desire the removal of every prejudice that proves a stumbling-block in the way of advancement.

He had accepted the argument of the 'Blue Books' that the Welsh language stood in the way of progress. That it must die might be 'intensely affecting' to the serious-minded, but it was subject to mutability like all other human affairs. Opponents to this *laissez-faire* attitude are castigated in the preface (*Not To Be Passed Over Unread*):

Certain parties in our principality, who may be designated the Fanatics of Welsh Nationality, have somewhat pertinaciously harped upon the question why I have written both this work and my 'Adventures and Vagaries of Twm Shôn Catty' in English rather than the Welsh vernacular. I might reply, although from my childhood acquainted with both languages, that a long residence in England, and a partiality for its language and literature had decided my preference. Such an announcement however would only provoke a rejoinder on the comparative antiquity, originality, and other imputed merits of the Welsh that would prove as interminable as unprofitable . . .

He goes on to say that, in addition to a personal preference for English, there is also the commercial consideration. The number of Welsh readers and book buyers is small and getting smaller, so that, *in these times, both authors and publishers are severe losers by such experiments as publishing books in the Welsh language.* He quotes an *eminent critic, William Taylor, of Norwich*, who urges that the inhabitants of *inconsiderable districts, such as Holland, Denmark, Piedmont, and Wales, should not endeavour to immortalize their respective phraseology, but contentedly slide into the speech of the larger contiguous nations.* As for political nationalism: *the final conquests of Wales and Scotland, and the union of Britain under one Sovereign* has proved *the greatest of blessings.* The *race-hatred* between Saxon and Celt he now pronounces *happily extinct . . . if we except certain slight instances generated principally by trade rivalry between the English settlers in Wales and the natives*, and some isolated cases

among the most rude and ignorant worshippers of the past, *who perversely turn their backs upon the sun of civilization and the onward velocity of the train of progress – wilfully blind to the inexpressible blessings of fraternal and national unity.*

On the language rule at the eisteddfod, he argues

that since the English speakers in Wales *contribute the greatest amount to these celebrations* and

those who . . . prefer Welsh exclusively, are numerically but a very insignificant minority, common sense, common justice, and the spirit of the age demand that a considerable portion of the Eisteddvod entertainments should be in the English language.

He vehemently condemns those who take an opposing view:

Those unreasonable, exclusive, and intemperate persons who manifest such repugnance to the dominant language of Britain, and insist on the propriety of every literary production competed for being only in the antiquated language of the principality of Wales, deserve to be stigmatized as the bigots and fanatics of Welsh nationality; who . . . are the very instruments who carry within themselves the destructive principle that sooner or later will destroy (Eisteddvodically speaking) their faith, creed, and ultimately the Eisteddvod itself.

How far these views were motivated by a deeply meditated conviction and how far by personal animosity is not now easy to assess, but it is quite certain that foremost among those here termed *the bigots and fanatics of Welsh nationality* were Lady Hall of Llanover and her circle. Whatever the motive, the final outcome for Prichard was a statement of policy, and a definition too, of what he called 'English-Welsh writing':

Happily the English writers of Wales, however opposed by the sticklers for the supremacy of the Welsh language, have met with due encouragement these many years past, and goodly fruit they have borne in the respective forms of learned and

48

interesting essays, in which the long neglected antiquities of Wales have undergone the most profound researches and critical examinations, while in the metrical department the poems and songs of the late Mrs. Hemans, John Humphry Parry [sic], and others, whose productions are entirely founded on the traditions and historic remains of Cambria, yield the fairest answers to all inquiries under those headings. And be it further observed, there is decidedly more Welsh nationality in an English production, when vigorously embracing the subject, historic or traditional, that is purely Cambrian, than in a composition in the Welsh language on affairs that are in no respect connected with Wales or Welshmen. Thus in reality, such English writers, after all cavilling, are by far the best supporters of Welsh literature . . .

By the time he had arrived at this conclusion – a basis for the establishment of a conscious school of writing, though it must see itself as antipathetic to literature in Welsh – Prichard's own career as a writer was over.

VI

Readers of Prichard's prose and poetry today will quickly become familiar with the people and political ideas he admires and those he condemns, but they will learn little directly about his life. Almost at the last gasp, he did make a clear statement about his birthplace. It occurs on page 536 of HEROINES OF WELSH HISTORY. There, in a chapter headed 'The Lady Matilda de Longpee', he is concerned to demonstrate his familiarity, and that of one of his sources, Theophilus Jones, an earlier historian of the county of Brecknock, with the landscape of the area where Llywelyn ap Gruffudd was killed. Parenthetically he writes:

(To impress the public with a full reliance on the accuracy of the account here presented, be it observed, Theophilus Jones was a native of the neighbourhood of Llangammarch village, six miles above the scene to be described; and the editor of the present work, of the town of Builth which is situated three miles below Cwm Llewelyn [sic].)

If Prichard was born in Builth and, to judge from particulars reported in the CAMBRIAN newspaper and contained in his death certificate, in 1790, then who was he? From what stock did he spring? In the eighteenth century, Builth was a thriving country town with resident tradespeople and licensees and a sprinkling from the ranks of the professions. Examination of the registers in the parish church of St Mary's reveals that Prichard (less often Pritchard, though both forms are sometimes employed in entries clearly referring to the same individual) is one of the commoner family names in the town from the 1750s and there is a notable increase in the incidence of such entries in the period 1790–1810. Unravelling the tangled skeins of baptisms, marriages and deaths is not made easier by the duplication of Christian names: Thomases, Davids and Catherines occur frequently. But none of the heads of families long resident in the town, whose occupations are described variously as glazier, hosier, farmer and fisherman, can present a serious claim to paternity of Prichard the writer and actor.

Such a claim can be made on behalf of another Prichard family that appears to have arrived in Builth in the late 1780s and to have stayed a relatively short time. The relevant entries in the registers read as follows:

1789
Thomas son of Thos. Pritchard Lawier Oct. 4th. Bapt.
1790
Thomas the son of Mr. Thos. Pritchard Atty. Burd. Jany. 6th.
Thos. Son of Thomas Prichard Lawyer Bapt. Oct. 29th by Anne his wife.
1791
Anne Dr. of Mr. Tho. Prichard Lawyer Bapt. Decr. 13th.
Anne Dr. of Thos. Prichard Lawyer Buried Decr. 27th.

No other certain signs of the family of Thomas and Anne Prichard survive in Builth. Though supporting evidence is lacking, it is not unreasonable to assume that Thomas Jeffery Llewelyn Prichard, the actor, writer and bookseller, is that Thomas, the second son so named, of 'Thomas Prichard Lawyer' and his wife

Anne, who was baptized on 29 October 1790. If Prichard's father was a lawyer, his own considerable education, which, as will be shown, seems to have included Latin and possibly some Greek, and his bookishness are understandable; it might even explain his love of the theatre.

No mention of the family occurs in the list of pew-holders at the parish church, an unusual circum-stance in view of Thomas Prichard's status. The reason for this must lie in enmity between the family and the Revd Benjamin Jones, who was vicar at the parish church of St Mary's from 1783 until 1825. The writer's attack on *the Rev. B- J-*, in the poems 'A Bishop a Thief, and a Parson a Clown' and 'Epigram', does not indicate the cause of the dispute, but it is tempting to think that a line in 'Ye Have Frowned', a highly personal section of that poetic rag-bag, 'The Noble of Nature', applies:

> *And shall I forget, while warm blood fills my veins?*
> *The slanderer whose venom my fair name would blot . . .*

Two further entries in the register might possibly throw light on the nature of the slander. On 31 March 1803, Vicar Jones noted, *Avarina reputata filia of Thos. Prichard Baptiz'd*, and on 25 January 1804 he wrote *Mary Anne reputed daughter of Thomas Prichard was baptiz'd*. Illegitimacy was not uncommon: few pages in the registers of Builth, Trallong and Llywel do not have at least one example and two or three is nearer the norm. Some of these entries refer to 'bastard' or 'base' child and to the mother as 'concubine' of the man identified as the father. No doubt public opprobrium attended such circum-stances and the reputation of a man of some standing in a locality could be damaged as a result. However, it is far from certain that the father of Avarina and Mary Anne was the same Thomas Prichard who, in the earlier entries quoted above, is invariably identified as a lawyer. At least one other Thomas Prichard, whose wife's name was Catherine, resided in Builth at this time.

Although the fabric of connecting evidence is thin, there are grounds for more than airy speculation about the writer's origins. From the subscribers' list to WELSH MINSTRELSY we know that Prichards were widely scattered and that some at least (like Mr Richard Prichard of Regent's Circus, London, and Mr Edward Prichard of Milford, Pembrokeshire) were in funds sufficient to purchase several copies of the book and give more than moral support to the author. That as Prichard or Pritchard, the family originated in Trallong, and that 'Thomas Prichard, lawyer' was himself from that area seems a strong possibility, not least because his wife Anne may well have been a Jeffreys, also from Trallong or the neighbouring parish of Llywel.

The evidence for this conjecture is bound up with Prichard's choice of a pen name. The use of pen-names was common among contributors to magazines in the 1820s, as the examples of Elia and Boz, and Welsh counterparts like Idrison and Brutus, remind us. But where did Prichard find 'Jeffery Llewelyn'? The answer is, close to home, for among the subscribers to WELSH MINSTRELSY we find another: the Revd Jeffery Llewelyn of Llywel. Today, Llywel is a hamlet just off the A40, between Senny-bridge and Llandovery, within a stone's throw of that cluster of locations – Rhyd y Briw, Trecastle,

Pentre-felin, Bryn-du, Llwyn-nyth and Defynnog – mentioned in Prichard's poems. The Jeffreys of Llywel, part of a large clan with many prominent members, had an estate called Bailie Cwmdwr in the more extensive parish of Llywel. When 'Rees Jeffreys, Gent.' died in 1810, he left to his 'nephews' Thomas Jeffreys and the Revd Rees Jeffreys, also of Llywel, a parcel of land and dwellings in the parish of Llanfihangel Nant Bran, and the responsibility of paying several small legacies

To David Jeffreys and Anne Jeffreys . . . the several sums of Twenty Pounds each . . . also to Rees Jeffreys Hugh Jeffreys William Jeffreys John Jeffreys and Anne Jeffreys the several sums of Five Pounds each.

But

All those Messuages Tenement and Dwellinghouses and Outhouses Stables gardens and other appurtenances in as large and ample manner as I now hold and enjoy same . . .

he bequeathed to the same Revd Jeffery Llewelyn, whom he also named sole executor. The will was proved, with considerable ado, at the Consistory Court in Brecon on 23 October 1810, an indication of discontent among some of the beneficiaries.

It is arguable that one or other of the Annes named in the will was Prichard's mother and that she and her son had been living at Bryn-du, a farm on the far western edge of the parish of Trallong conveniently close to a wealthy and ageing relative. This conjecture would be strengthened if it could be demonstrated that, about 1800, Bryn-du was owned or tenanted by Jeffreys kin. Land Tax Assessments show that William Jeffreys and Walter Jeffreys owned properties in the parish of Trallong in 1798, but, frustratingly, they do not say which. However, the additional fact that, when the tithe map was drawn up in 1840, Thomas Jeffreys was the occupant of Bryn-du is fairly persuasive. Five pounds, or even twenty, would have been scant reward for Anne's show of family loyalty. Here would be reason enough for the writer's various allusions to poverty and exile, and his scathing (if indirect) criticism of the rich who ignore the claims of impoverished relatives and dispose of their estates to others already wealthy. Prichard's choice of Jeffery Llewelyn as *nom de plume* becomes in this light still hopeful flattery, or satire, or both. That it cut no ice with the reverend gentleman, who survived until 1834, is demonstrated by his purchase of a single copy of WELSH MINSTRELSY, where he might have read (in 'Ye Have Frowned!', mentioned above):

> *Ye have frowned on my hopes, and my claims ye reject,*
> *Ye have frowned on my hopes – yet I dare stand erect –*
> *Now your glance cannot awe, nor your smilings elate,*
> *Too proud is my heart, though despising to hate . . .*

Prichard begins his preface to WELSH MINSTRELSY thus:

Since I commenced the most difficult part of my undertaking – that of travelling to seek subscribers to this work – in compliment to the taste of my own country people, to whom I have been estranged since boyhood, the nature of the publication has been almost thoroughly changed . . .

The emphasis is mine. How much of his boyhood was spent in or near Builth and at Bryn-du remains a matter for conjecture since no record of the family exists, in Builth or elsewhere, beyond 1791. For the next positive identification we have to wait until the summer of 1820, when the first of his poems appeared in the sixth number of the CAMBRO-BRITON. That Prichard was living in London and had probably done so for a considerable time becomes clear from the subscribers' list to WELSH MINSTRELSY, which shows that he had a wide circle of acquaintance there.

There is no clue to his schooling, or whether he was trained for a profession. He might have been intended for accountancy, as his last recorded word – to the census enumerator in 1861 – suggests. (Or, given his state of destitution, was that an example of self-lacerating irony? Or was his snuffled response simply misheard and wrongly recorded?) His writing and his considerable stock of learning suggest that he received a substantial education that might well have included a grounding in the classics. In a note to 'The Sevi-Lan-Gwy', intended to defend the Welsh language against detractors who *deem it uncouth*, Prichard compares Welsh with Homer's Greek, a language *no less guttural and no more energetic*. He illustrates his point by considering the pronunciation of 'Achilles' in Welsh, which in its 'ch' preserves the sound of the original Greek more effectively than English. Lord Chesterfield, he further comments, *has deservedly ridiculed the mincing names of the Grecian heroes in French translations*. It is possible then that he had at least a superficial knowledge of the Greek alphabet, though he might equally well have taken his cue in this case, as in so many others, from a series of learned articles on Welsh and its similarities to other languages, particularly Hebrew, Greek and Latin, in the CAMBRO-BRITON. There is no reference in the CAMBRO-BRITON to Lord Chesterfield, the man who famously earned Dr Samuel Johnson's rebuke for neglecting him and, perhaps more famously, maintained an educational and affectionate correspondence with his illegitimate son, which was first published in 1774. It was in one of these letters that Prichard read:

> *wherever custom and usage will allow it, I would rather chuse*
> *not to alter the ancient proper names. They have more dignity, I*
> *think, in their own, than in our language. The French change*
> *most of the ancient proper names, and give them a French*
> *termination or ending, which sometimes sounds even*
> *ridiculous; as, for instance, they call the Emperor Titus, Tite . . .*
> *(Letter XVI)*

He was also familiar with the writing of the dissipated cleric and poet Charles Churchill (1731–64), who exercised his gifts as a satirist to escape from poverty. He is mentioned, and extensively quoted, on the first page of WELSH MINSTRELSY, in the dedication to the Bishop of St David's, which praises *the manly plainness of Churchill's dedication to the Bishop of Gloucester, equally removed from servility as untruth.* Churchill first found fame and considerable wealth on the publication of THE ROSCIAD (1761), a satire on actors, which may have brought his energetic style and mordant wit to Prichard's attention. He was a model that the ever impecunious Prichard could have wished to emulate, and that Byron admired Churchill was a further recommendation. Elements of Augustanism are clearly present in Prichard's prosody, though (as we have seen) he dismissed that *starch school.* He had also read his Romantic contemporaries and preferred them *to any that have graced the country, since the setting of the glorious star of Tudor – the great Shakespearian age,* and there is plentiful evidence of his allegiance to their liberal ideals, and of his ambition to emulate their achievements.

In addition to whatever formal education he had received, Prichard had taken pains to educate himself. Epigraphs to poems and occasional quotations in WELSH MINSTRELSY are drawn from Shakespeare (RICHARD III, A WINTER'S TALE, ROMEO AND JULIET), from Chaucer, Cowper's Homer, Coleridge, Byron and the Bible. In notes on the poems he acknowledges an array of sources: 'Morris's Survey', 'Carlisle's Topographical Dictionary', 'Meyrick's Cardigan', 'Camden's Britannia', 'Bingley's North Wales', 'Cambrian Biography', 'Fuller's Worthies', 'Giraldus', 'Pennant', 'History of the Gwydir family', 'Picture of Monmouthshire'. A few of the epigraphs, which he must have quoted from memory, have inaccuracies, but the list indicates a considerable breadth of reading. Perhaps the clearest evidence of his bookishness and his love of language is his garnering of odd and archaic words from Johnson's DICTIONARY. A good sprinkling of lines throughout WELSH MINSTRELSY are impenetrable without recourse to Johnson. Words such as 'appetible', 'tarriance', and 'contristate', though unusual, might be guessed at and are understandable in their context, 'palmipede' (web-footed) may well be recognized by zoologists, but what can the reader make of 'glike' (sneer, scoff), which even Johnson says is *not now in use*, of 'absterse' (cleanse), 'acclivious' (sloping), 'immarcessible' (unfading), 'marcid' (withered), 'calid' (fervent), 'macilent' (lean), 'fatidical' (prophetic) and so on? This vocabulary is often Latinate, and that might indicate a familiarity with the Latin roots of words. It is also possible that Prichard learned them first in plays of the seventeenth and eighteenth centuries, along with the fustian and declamatory style of much of his writing, unlike that of the Romantic contemporaries for whom he expressed admiration.

The principal source of his information about Welsh culture is unacknowledged, other than cryptically in a note on 'Welsh Biddings', which quotes at length from an account of this traditional practice *addressed to the editor of a periodical work*. The editor was John Humffreys Parry, the periodical, the CAMBRO-BRITON. That he read and used other journals of the period, again without acknowledgement, is clear from the translation of 'Hanes Taliesin' / 'The History of Taliesin' included among the notes to WELSH MINSTRELSY. The text in this case, printed in double column as in the source, is volume II of the TRANSACTIONS OF THE HONOURABLE SOCIETY OF CYMMRODORION (1828). The editor of the first volume had been the same John Humffreys Parry, elected to that role in 1822, the year in which the CAMBRO-BRITON ceased publication due to lack of support. Items first published in the latter were subsequently reprinted in the TRANSACTIONS. Parry was a writer, editor and antiquary of considerable talent, as his namesake John Parry (Bardd Alaw) admitted in a letter to William Jenkins Rees, the rector of Cascob, but a man with 'oddities' and perhaps frequently 'tipsy' – attributes that may have led to his undoing. He died of a blow he received from one William Bennett, in Long Street, Pentonville outside The Prince of Wales tavern on 12 February 1825. But the omission of any reference to his name or his journal was probably not due to Parry's untimely death: the contents of WELSH MINSTRELSY had been composed at least a year or so earlier. Prichard usually neglected, or forgot, to express in print his indebtedness to his most generous benefactor, the same rector of Cascob, for assisting his literary endeavours. The absence of reference to Parry appears wilful. The reason may lie in Prichard's relationship with the CAMBRO-BRITON. From the editor's messages to Jeffery Llewelyn in his 'Notices' column, and the probable editorial amendment of the two poems that appeared in the magazine, we gain an impression of Prichard's importunity and Parry's coolness. There was, one would guess, an entire absence of mutual regard.

Nevertheless, he gained a great deal from the CAMBRO-BRITON, including (whenever he remembered) the Welsh orthography favoured by Parry who, in the November 1821 issue of his magazine, offered *a few words in defence of a peculiarity, which will, in future, distinguish the Cambro-Briton . . . We allude to the substitution, in all Welsh words, of the v and f for f and ff, so preposterously introduced and so obstinately retained in our modern orthography.* In this particular, Prichard became more radical later in his career, substituting 'sh' for 'si' (Siôn becomes Shôn), 'y' for 'i' (Catti becomes Catty), and employing 'aa' for 'â' as in 'Shaan'. This may be a concession to a potential English audience, but is also possibly an expression of revolt against supporters of a pristine Welsh when his own early enthusiasm for the language waned.

VII

What was Prichard doing to support himself while he was failing to impress John Humffreys Parry? In all probability he was making a living on the stage. That he had theatrical connections is clear from the subscribers' list to WELSH MINSTRELSY, which includes Mr C. Baker of the Theatre Royal, Covent Garden in London, Mr Hastings and Mr John Haines of the Coburg Theatre (later the Old Vic), Mr Frederick Mortimer of the Theatre Royal, Brighton, and Mr Macready of the Theatre Royal, Bristol. Charles Macready became a star; more usually associated with Drury Lane and Covent Garden, he also found time to tour the provinces. John Thomas Haines was both actor and playwright; Charles Baker had a reputation as a comedian. Frederick Mortimer is another known actor of the period, but there is no record of Mr Hastings – or indeed of Thomas Prichard, or Jeffery Llewelyn, or any combination of those names.

However, as early as 1814 another name with strong Breconshire connections begins to appear regularly in Covent Garden playbills: 'Mr Jefferies'. He is clearly a regular, if minor, member of the company with small roles in many productions. He plays Benvolio in ROMEO AND JULIET; Bernardo in HAMLET; Lennox in MACBETH; Gonzalo in THE TEMPEST; Trebonius in JULIUS CAESAR. In Otway's VENICE PRESERVED he is Captain of the Guard, in ZAMBUCA, a spearguard, and in TOM THUMB THE GREAT, he is

Merlin. Whenever these productions, and a good many others, are revived (the Shakespearean plays regularly) in the period 1814–22, Mr Jefferies has his role. In 1820 and 1821, he has small parts in plays by the elder and the younger George Colman – barely known now but, as his poem 'Drama's Petition' shows, well regarded as dramatists by Prichard. In the November 1822 revival of ROMEO AND JULIET, Benvolio is played by that Mr Baker whose name we have noted above, and there is no sign of Jefferies until he returns on 16 December 1822 to perform once more as Captain of the Guard in VENICE PRESERVED. He continues then in his usual roles until 23 June 1823, when he plays Vibulanus in another play now forgotten, VIRGINIUS, OR THE LIBERATION OF ROME. After this performance his name disappears, and the parts that had been his for eight or more years passed to Mr Baker and several other actors.

Could 'Mr Jefferies' be another name adopted by Prichard? Circumstantial evidence would support the notion. If the Jeffreys connection through his mother is accepted, the choice of name is itself significant, and chronology plays a part. Some time in 1822 Prichard arranged the printing of his first pamphlet, MY LOWLY LOVE, with William Phillips of Worthing. In 1823, MARIETTE MOULINE was printed in London. We might reasonably assume that sales of the pamphlets funded his removal to Wales in 1823, where he toured extensively, especially in the counties of the south, soliciting subscriptions to WELSH MINSTRELSY from door to door. The book was published in 1824, to begin his career as writer. The dates match the pattern of stage performances by Mr Jefferies.

There is no evidence that, during the six weeks or so towards the end of 1822 he was absent from the Theatre Royal, Covent Garden, Mr Jefferies was in Worthing; the season at the Theatre Royal there had finished that year in October. The subscribers' list shows Prichard knew Frederick Mortimer at the Theatre Royal in the neighbouring town, Brighton, but no playbills of that theatre have survived for the period in question. What we have in the end is in the realm of inspired guess, or forlorn hope. Yet Prichard *did* know the theatre, wrote a pamphlet of THEATRICAL POEMS, now lost, impressed people in Wales with his extensive knowledge of the London stage, and, according to the 'Bye-Gones' correspondents, took to the boards again.

In 1823, Prichard set out on his own account to make a living out of literature. He followed the well-tried practice of issuing a prospectus advertising a more substantial book and inviting purchase by subscription. This he could have learned from Dr Johnson, or any number of eighteenth-century writers, but if he had a particular model in mind, it was probably Parry and his magazine. Subscribers were urged to enrol at *Mr. Limbird's, Printer and Publisher, 355 Strand*, where the CAMBRO-BRITON had been printed.

The prospectus is interesting for what it conveys about Prichard. He writes of *his wayward and humble fortunes continually thwarting and preventing his intentions* to publish; of MARIETTE MOULINE, which *was so fortunate to meet the approbation of some who are highly capable of estimating poetic labour;* of the encouraging response purchasers gave to the preface of that booklet, which he quotes from at length; and he re-emphasizes his intention henceforth to write on Welsh subjects rather than English.

A footnote adds that, in some quarters (*whether in compliment or derision, is immaterial*), he is known as 'The Welsh Bloomfield'. Robert Bloomfield (1766–1823), a farm labourer from Suffolk, achieved a measure of fame and a considerable fortune from the publication of THE FARMER'S BOY (1800). He subsequently wrote (at tedious length) THE BANKS OF THE WYE: A POEM IN FOUR BOOKS (1811), following a walking tour that had taken him from Chepstow as far as Brecon and back via Hereford in 1807. This might have been inspirational, but was more likely galling to another writer born on the banks of the Wye. One might speculate that it is more than mere coincidence that both Prichard in Canto III of 'The Land Beneath the Sea' and Bloomfield in Book IV of THE BANKS OF THE WYE write about the Welsh custom of decking graves with flowers. In any event, while Prichard would have envied the other's success, he clearly resents the comparison with Bloomfield. His implied sense of superiority over the farm labourer may have derived from the common knowledge that Bloomfield's spelling and grammar needed the careful attention of his editor, Capel Lofft, but at this point in the prospectus he issues a bold, or foolhardy, challenge:

Ignorant indeed must I be of human nature and the spirit of the times, could I not anticipate that I shall be censured for imprudence and egotism . . . and that I thus invite the severity of criticism: be it so! with no less severity stand I self-measured with Poets who have succeeded, without the aid of great connections, or fawning sycophancy towards the powerful and wealthy . . .

It is somewhat Johnsonian in pride and professional-
ism of purpose. Prichard is a pioneer among Anglo-
Welsh writers who set out to earn a living by the
pen. He could hardly have anticipated the hardship
his career choice would bring. In 1823, he looked
back on past disappointments and, for the moment,
forward with determination:

*Too long have my MSS. been left to moulder, too many lost, and
too often have I hawked them from Publisher to Publisher, to
continue longer the humble maudlin modesty that hitherto has
proved but invitations to the cold-blooded insults of purse-
proud trafficking stupidity . . . One novelty, at least, I dare
promise to my future readers – the productions of A
WELSHMAN, who wishes always to be identified as such, with
a most decided contempt of the system of anglofying, or
classification with the English, to the denial of their mother
land, a habit too prevalent among my countrymen, who become
fortunate in England.*

The prospectus bears the name T. Jeffery Llewelyn
Prichard, rather than the pen-name he had become
accustomed to using. It was perhaps another signal
that he was reclaiming his Welsh roots. Later this
was to change again to T. J. Llewelyn Prichard. There
is a hint of desperation as well as defiance in the
writing. He was turning his back on the stage and
the London-Welsh literary establishment. What hope
he had of future prosperity lay in Wales. By the time
the book was published in 1824, the subscription list
to WELSH MINSTRELSY contained 867 names; only
forty-six had addresses outside Wales, the vast
majority of these in London. At seven shillings a
copy, the project should have brought him a little
more than £300, before the deduction of printing,
travelling and other expenses. Bloomfield, whose

FARMER'S BOY sold 26,000 copies in three years, had done rather better.

As we have seen, he takes the part of the players, notably in 'Drama's Petition' and TWM SHÔN CATTI against the *rude and sullen Bigotry* of Methodism that condemned them as harbingers of vice. This is echoed in a story about Prichard by another 'Bye-Gones' correspondent (March 1882) styling himself 'Ceredig Cyfeiliog', who was writing in response to the earlier note by F. S. A. quoted at the beginning of this essay. He relates how it was impossible for the company that Prichard was touring with in Aberystwyth in the 1840s to find a printer who would produce playbills because *theatrical performances were* [considered to be] *emphatically and exclusively in the interests of the prince of darkness*. In the end, some redundant types were obtained, the text was set and, in the absence of a press, the weight of an actor of substantial proportions called Crutchley was employed to print the bills. He goes on to claim that Prichard's performances in the Assembly Rooms at Aberystwyth *are well remembered by many of the inhabitants*.

Twenty years or so earlier the writer had been in Brecon at the same time as Charles Crisp's touring company, and like certain members of the company had enjoyed the hospitality of Captain Frederick Jones, a man of considerable wealth and culture, who kept a diary. On 20 October 1824 he recorded: *Dinner at Major Prices. And all to ye Play, being ye opening of ye House. 'School for Scandal'.*; on 30 October: *Geoffry Lewel Prichard dined ch.n.* [chez-nous], and 10 November: *T. Geofry Lewellyn Prichard ye Poet ch.m.* [chez-moi] *N.B.* The third entry suggests it was not as an associate of Crisp's company, but in the guise of poet and subscription seller that Prichard visited Captain Jones – as the subscribers' list to WELSH MINSTRELSY testifies, for there his name is marked with an asterisk, to acknowledge receipt of hospitality, and he took two copies.

What made the 10 November visit notable one is left to guess. Could it have been something to do with the nose? (Though in that case dinner on 30 October would have been equally memorable.) Whether or not the nose had a part in it, the account of Prichard by Charles Wilkins, the postmaster, librarian and journalist of Merthyr Tydfil, in CYMRY FU (1889) probably explains why Captain Jones, who was an enthusiast for all things theatrical, invited him 'chez-moi' a second time:

My earliest recollection of Llewelyn Prichard was in finding him sitting near me in a dramatic entertainment at Merthyr, and listening to a long string of remembrances of old players and old authors. It was as if a nightly habitué of by-gone Sadler's Wells had come to life, familiar with the stage and its annals from Shakespeare and Ben Jonson down to the days of Beaumont, Fletcher, Dryden, and Sheridan, and able to give varied quotations from celebrated players as well as from all the poets from Savage and Churchill to Cowper, Southey, and Crabbe, and a host beside. He was gaunt and grey, with thin features and lustrous eyes, a false nose – having lost his natural one in a fencing match – and he spoke with an earnest snuffle – I say this kindly – from which most people would quickly have turned away . . .

This encounter occurred during the period when Prichard was selling HEROINES OF WELSH HISTORY. He was in his sixties and fast approaching the final decline that would deposit him, destitute, at World's End, Swansea. In another part of his account in

'Bye-Gones', 'Ceredig Cyfeiliog' describes meeting the writer perhaps a decade earlier, while he was employed by the then Lady Augusta Hall to compile a catalogue of the books in her library at Llanover:

During the time to which I am referring I used to meet him almost daily either at his task among the books or strolling in the charming grounds that surround the mansion, and he appeared then as a person that had seen better days . . . [He] had the artificial nose alluded to when I met him at Llanover; but it did not then look so very amiss. I remember his once humorously remarking that the second artist was not nearly equal to the first in the matter of nose-making.

A report of court proceedings in the CAMBRIAN newspaper, 8 August 1856, tells how a navvy was jailed for one month for biting off another's nose during a violent affray in High Street, Swansea, and how Mr Michael, the surgeon, *very skilfully made an artificial 'Grecian' organ, which being carefully adjusted defies the scrutiny of the closest observer.* This is not Prichard, of course, but the circumstances described must be commoner in the annals of lost noses, and the testimony to the surgeon's skill is interesting. At a little distance, a wax prosthesis may not have appeared untoward – as 'Ceredig Cyfeiliog' also testifies. When and how Prichard lost his nose remains a mystery. Injury in a fencing match might be thought a hazard of the acting profession. A well-advertised *celebrated combat of six* in the forgotten play HORATII AND CURIATII that appears in Covent Garden playbills about 1820 would seem to afford the right circumstances for chance mutilation. If one supposes that loss of a nose would end any kind of stage career, then Prichard still possessed his original in the early 1840s, when it is said he acted at Brecon and Aberystwyth. In the few letters that have survived, Prichard refers to long, life-threatening illness. That too is a possible cause of disfigurement, but the fencing match is a better story.

The only strictly contemporary record of Prichard's appearance in the 1820s is tantalizingly equivocal. On 22 September 1826, David Rice Rees, who was a bookseller and kept the Post at Llandovery, wrote to his brother, William Jenkins Rees at Cascob:

Mr Llewellyn [sic] *Prichard called, in his way (on foot) to Carmarthen, he dined here . . . he was prevailed upon by the manager of the Llandovery Theatre to perform one night, which he did & left town early next morning. His appearance did not strike me as being very prepossessing . . .*

Was Prichard ill-clothed, unkempt and dusty from his travels on foot, or was there a plainer reason for his unprepossessing appearance? And assuming Rees witnessed the stage performance, why did he not comment upon it?

While little is known of Prichard's personal history in his most productive years as a poet, 1819 to 1824, there are several significant indications of the literature and the political beliefs that influenced him. As we have seen, Prichard admired Charles Churchill and would have known that he was a close associate of John Wilkes (1727–97), best remembered now as the great campaigner for freedom of the press and the foremost representative of liberal causes of his time. Prichard also professed the *most decided and hearty admiration for the living race of writers*. That he meant the major poets who were his closest contemporaries, Shelley (1792–1822), Keats

(1795–1821) and Byron (1788–1824), as well as the somewhat older liberal thinker Coleridge (1772–1834), is immediately apparent from his choice of 'publisher' for WELSH MINSTRELSY: John and H. L. Hunt of Tavistock Street, Covent Garden, an address close to the Theatre Royal. The book was printed by John Cox in Aberystwyth and what the Hunts (father and son) had to do with its production is open to question. It was important to Prichard that the book should be seen to have the imprimatur of a London publisher and an obvious choice would have been Limbird, who published the CAMBRO-BRITON and was collecting subscriptions for WELSH MINSTRELSY. Given the climate of the times, the selection of John and H. L. Hunt was a political statement.

In 1808, John Hunt, the journal's founder, was joined on the weekly EXAMINER by his younger brother (James Henry) Leigh Hunt. In 1813 they were prosecuted for publishing a libel on the Prince Regent, whom they had characterized as:

a violator of his word, a libertine over head and ears in disgrace, a despiser of domestic ties, the companion of gamblers and demi-reps, a man who has just closed half a century without a single claim on the gratitude of his country or the respect of posterity.

They were sentenced to two years' imprisonment, which they served in separate gaols, and each fined £500. Leigh Hunt continued to edit the periodical from prison and its independent, radical stance did not alter. In his even more radical journal, YELLOW DWARF, John Hunt hoisted the banner of the movement for 'Universal Suffrage and Annual Parliaments' and warned the government:

persecute and murder away: you cannot kill us all; and if you will use the bayonet, we must make up our minds to the quantity of suffering you can inflict; we shall soon see whether brute force or mind shall triumph . . .

These lines appeared in May 1818, on the page facing the first printing of Keats's 'Hymn to Pan'. The Hunts were committed supporters of Keats, who has recently been shown to have shared their radical views – the principal reason for the virulence of the attacks he suffered at the hands of BLACKWOOD'S and the QUARTERLY magazine. Shelley, whose NECESSITY OF ATHEISM had caused consternation at Oxford and Worthing, left England in the same year, in part at least because he feared he would be prosecuted for his anti-government views. His 'Hymn to Intellectual Beauty' had been published in the EXAMINER in January 1817, and 'The Mask of Anarchy', his white-hot response to news from England of what became known as the Peterloo Massacre, was also intended for the same weekly in the autumn of 1819, but Leigh Hunt withheld it until 1832 because of the near certainty at the time that its publisher would be prosecuted and severely punished.

Byron's poem 'Windsor Poetics', satirizing the Prince Regent with characteristic wit, had been written in April 1813. He too held radical political views and frequently visited Leigh Hunt during his two years in prison. In 1821, Shelley wrote from Italy to propose that Leigh Hunt should join with him and Byron to found a new journal. The outcome was the LIBERAL. Shelley was already dead (as was Keats) by the time the first number appeared in 1822. It included Byron's 'The Vision of Judgement', which his usual publisher Murray would not touch. For publishing this work *calumniating the late King, and wounding the feelings of his present majesty* John Hunt was fined £100. It was Hunt too, rather than Murray, who published the last eleven cantos of Byron's satirical epic 'Don Juan'. Hazlitt dedicated his collected POLITICAL ESSAYS to John Hunt, whom he praised as *the tried, steady, zealous, and conscientious advocate of the liberty of his country and the rights of mankind.*

These then were the turbulent times during which Prichard was attempting to establish himself as a writer; John Hunt was the radical publisher whose name he chose to have on the title page of his first substantial book and, by extension, Keats, Shelley and, unquestionably, Byron were the representatives of the *living race of writers* for whom he professed the *most decided and hearty admiration,* as much for their political opinions as their art. We have seen how Prichard's liberal, humane and proletarian views inspired polemical poems like 'The Star of Liberty' and 'The Woes of the Cottage', and several prose passages condemning the neglect of the rural poor. Justifiably, in the aftermath of the Napoleonic Wars, he wrote of *Europe's sons of blood, / The homicidal viper brood!*

There is enough in Prichard's published work to establish his alignment with the radical group he admired on the broad issues of human rights. Towards the end of his life (in the letter of 1857 quoted by Charles Wilkins) he claimed he was writing satire – *Raps at the Russians (struck principally during the late war) in a series of epigrams, satirettes, and other petite missives* – and among the pile of manuscripts that the kindly gentleman of Swansea discovered in Prichard's pitiful dwelling in 1861 was that entitled 'Medallions of the Memorable', *in a series of historic essays and sonnets,* which seems to promise a return to the broader political view. Nothing of these survives.

VIII

Prichard returned to Wales with hopes of improved success by writing for his own people. On Wales and the Welsh language he was outspoken in verse and prose, though his views changed dramatically. In his dedication of WELSH MINSTRELSY to the Bishop of St David's he wrote of *the strong feelings of nationality, so peculiar to a Welshman* and praised the Bishop for his

cultivation of their native language . . . the tongue of our forefathers, the language of the brave and the free . . . venerable for its antiquity, no less flexible than powerfully impressive, that in spite of all the elements combined for its destruction, has survived the wreck of ages.

In the prospectus to the CAMBRIAN BALNEA, dated 1825, he claimed the motive for the work was a *passionate desire to rescue from unmerited obscurity whatever relates to Wales.* We have seen how, while still preserving an interest in its history and culture, by the 1850s, when he was concluding his work on HEROINES OF WELSH HISTORY, he was pleased to see Wales absorbed into Britain and the Welsh language in what he assumed to be terminal decline.

In 1823–4, Prichard settled in Aberystwyth, found a printer, John Cox, in Great Dark-Gate Street, saw WELSH MINSTRELSY (rather carelessly) through the press, and continued his efforts to sell the book, often from town to town and door to door. He explored Aberystwyth and the surrounding countryside, sampled the 'season' and its entertainments, learned about the local landowners, their deeds and misdeeds. This was the most promising and productive period of his life: it would not last. THE ABERYSTWYTH GUIDE and his final pamphlet of poems, ABERYSTWYTH IN MINIATURE, also appeared in 1824. There is a cheerful confidence about these productions, most clearly expressed in 'The Drama's Petition', very different from the defensively haughty posturing of the prefaces to his earlier publications. Out of, what may be assumed, the success of THE ABERYSTWYTH GUIDE came the initiative to compile a LLANDRINDOD GUIDE and, with that, the grand idea of a work to be published in parts embracing spa towns and villages throughout Wales. If they had all received an influx of visitors comparable to Aberystwyth, and if Prichard had been able to deliver parts regularly on the scale the prospectus for the work promised, the future of the journal might have been assured.

The publishers of the LLANDRINDOD GUIDE/CAMBRIAN BALNEA are, ostensibly, John and H. L. Hunt, but various copies bear the names of different printers and have differing title pages, some dated 1825, some undated. The differences suggest Prichard travelled widely in south Wales carrying partly made-up copies of the text that he had bound only when there were sales to justify the expense. It can be safely assumed he was no longer based in Aberystwyth. Indeed, in 1825 begins the only extant record of Prichard's movements in letters in his own hand. This has come about by the doubly fortunate circumstance of his finding both a supporter and an indefatigable hoarder of papers of all descriptions in Revd William Jenkins Rees. They might possibly have met previously, for both had connections, albeit tenuous on Prichard's part, with the CAMBRO-BRITON, and the rector of Cascob did occasionally sojourn in London. Although he was not a listed subscriber, Rees knew of WELSH MINSTRELSY, as he did the CAMBRIAN BALNEA, because he had received and retained the prospectuses. In any event, Prichard's first letter, written from Hay on 9 March 1825, is a curious blend of the formal and informal:

I intend to do myself the pleasure of giving you a call between this and Sunday next, at Cascob. I have been to see Llanerch-goedlan Well, but I am much disappointed, as it is the weakest Sulphur water that I have met with. Notwithstanding the desires of some of the great, who patronize this Spa, and wish to trumpet it into celebrity, I must decline being their pipe on the occasion, as my duty to the public, whose confidence & patronage I wish to earn honestly, must claim from me a record of contrary tendency.

A portion of my MS has been lost for two months, by my present printer Mr. Nicholas of Newport, but was found about a week ago, & I shall very shortly have 2 numbers more of the work out. I hope to get a few Subscribers at Presteigne and Kington. I heartily hope to find you well, and believe me, / My Dear Sir, / Yours very truly / T. J. Llewelyn Prichard

Whereas the making of the Aberystwyth and Llandrindod guides had been simplified by the availability of previously published texts, the waters of less-publicized spas appear to have required first-hand sampling. Travel, to obtain subscriptions as well as for research, meant expense and less time for writing, added to which there was the perennial problem of finding efficient and accommodating printers. In these circumstances the long-term goals of the project were difficult to sustain. Prichard decided that travel costs had to be reduced: in a sad postscript to his letter he explained, *As I am now on foot, I cannot name the precise day when I shall be able to reach Cascob.* From this time he also began to rely upon the kindness, good offices and extensive library of William Jenkins Rees.

Prichard's struggle to keep the project alive into the autumn of 1825 proved futile, despite the advertised promise in some copies of the LLANDRINDOD GUIDE to provide a miscellany of more interesting items, including

several select biographical notices, including those of the notorious Twm Siôn Catti; a description of his Cave; with a detail of his knavish exploits, partly translated from the Welsh *and now first collected.*

The emphasis is mine. Prichard's next letter to Cascob, dated 29 October 1825, and written from Merthyr Tydfil, explains the source of the translation and how Prichard had himself been pursuing enquiries into Twm Siôn Catti. He begins with an apology for not replying sooner to two communications from Rees, one of which contained an *account of Llandovery*, no doubt solicited as a contribution to the Balnea, *so copious, original and interesting* as to leave him *as much astonished as gratified.* He promised to make due acknowledgement of its source but, as with later gifts of this kind from Cascob, failed to do so:

Soon after I had the pleasure of seeing you at Llandovery, I took a ride over from Llanwrtyd across the mountain to Twm Sion Catti's cave, of which, with an account of my ride there I mean to give a description in the Balnea. I am very anxious to collect information and the floating anecdotes respecting this popular Welsh freebooter. Would you be so good, at your leisure, as to translate the enclosed, and keep the original for me? . . . I should like to know on what authority he is considered to have ended his days as a magistrate of Breconshire. It seems he was contemporary with Owen Glyndwr – Do you know anything of his history, or the traditions respecting him?

The letter conveys Prichard's hazy notion of chronology, and a good deal more about his indebtedness to Rees. Unexpectedly, it also tells us that he was unable to speak, or at least, to read and translate Welsh, notwithstanding his public patriotism and, at this time, espousal of the language cause. It is certain that 'the enclosed' was an eight-page pamphlet, Y DIGRIFWR / CASGLIAD O GAMPIAU A DICHELLION THOMAS JONES, O DREGARON YN ABERTEIFI / *Yr hwn sydd yn cael ei adnabod yn gyffredin wrth yr enw / Twm Siôn Catti*, which was published in 1811 – without naming it, he admitted as much in his preface to the 'novel' he penned a year or so later. Had he but known, Prichard could have saved himself the trouble of writing and the good rector his leisure, for Y DIGRIFWR is itself a translation of part of an earlier, anonymous pamphlet in English, THE JOKER; OR MERRY COMPANION / TO WHICH ARE ADDED / TOMSHONE CATTY'S TRICKS, printed by J. Ross and R. Thomas in Carmarthen in 1763.

We do not know how quickly Rees supplied the translation. However, the BALNEA project continued to lose momentum until Prichard was forced to concede it was a lost cause. The times were not propitious for an undertaking of this kind; the great majority of Prichard's countrymen were as impoverished as he. In the period following the end of the war against Napoleon, economic depression afflicted town and country, manufacturing and farming; it was particularly severe and unremitting in the countryside. John Davies's A HISTORY OF WALES describes the worsening conditions for agriculture, the mainstay of the majority of people, the decline in incomes of landowners and their tenants, and the poverty of the hired hands. Landowners tried to offset their losses by maintaining rents at levels tenants could no longer afford:

In consequence, almost every estate recorded a massive increase in arrears in the years immediately following the war. Arrears rose again in 1826, when ready money was in short supply because of the banking crisis of 1825–6. In the course of that crisis, many of the banks that had been established in the market towns of Wales from 1760 onwards failed.

On 4 April 1826, Prichard wrote to Rees from an address at *Widemarsh Gate Hereford* about his attempts to sort out some unsatisfactory business with a printer on Rees's behalf, and his own affairs. He has been unwell and *thrown . . . into considerable difficulties* [by a] *stoppage of the Banks . . . which to a person possessed of little, and that little in Hereford Notes is a serious inconvenience.* He thanks Rees profusely for the contrasting hospitality he enjoyed at *the happy Rectory in the peaceful valley of Cascob* and especially for the assistance his host gave him *in extracting from your rare and valuable books.* Some he must have borne away with him, for he has been busy transcribing *nearly all from your books except Churchyard's 'Worthines of Wales.' I find I shall have to copy the greater part of the whole of that book, which is no trifling matter.* Thomas Churchyard (1520?–1604), like Prichard, tramped the highways and byways, earnestly striving to make a living by the pen. Churchyard's book, a long descriptive poem about the history and geography of Wales, might well have been fodder for the BALNEA, but Prichard writes also of *great anticipations from the success of the projected work, as well as my present undertaking*, which suggests he had discussed another project with Rees, almost certainly a history, and was already collecting materials for it.

In the same letter he refers to his wife, whom he will send to Builth while he undertakes another errand on Rees's behalf and, as though by-the-by, a further change in his personal circumstances:

My amiable and worthy Girl, whom I have so lately made my wife was much gratified when I explained to her the cause of my long stay at your house, and hopes to be enabled, some time, to thank you personally. We have fixed on a decided Cambrian name for our child, (secretly be it whispered, and only to the ear of a friend, that we have one already!) what do you think of Tydvil Nest Prichard?

He had married Naomi James at Abergavenny on 13 January 1826. In the 1841 census, when Naomi and five of her children, but not her husband, were living in High Street, Builth, her age is given as thirty, though since it was usual in that census for ages above fifteen to be rounded down, she could have been thirty to thirty-four. The higher figure is more consistent with the evidence (from the Builth register) that she was forty at the time of her death in 1848. At her marriage she was eighteen or there-abouts. In 1826, 'home' was not Abergavenny but Builth. Prichard's enemy in the town, the Revd Benjamin Jones, had recently died, but with the bride in an advanced state of pregnancy it would have been more discreet to marry in another town. News of the event was published in the CAMBRIAN and, as we have seen, in SEREN GOMER, in each case the groom being described as the author of WELSH MINSTRELSY. Their daughter Tydvil was born in Hereford: her baptism is recorded in the parish of All Saints on 26 March 1826 (where her father, eschewing common trades or professions, rather grandly declared himself a 'Gentleman') and it seems likely that Hereford was Naomi's birthplace. She was literate (the birth certificate of her son, Llewelyn Felix, bears her neat signature), and she had a trade: she was a milliner. Marriage did not set a term on Prichard's gypsy life. As the letter indicates, he had spent some time at Cascob in the weeks preceding the birth of his daughter and he continued to travel, gathering material and selling his books or soliciting subscriptions.

The next letter from Prichard preserved by the Revd William Jenkins Rees came from an address in Cross Street, Builth (where, he says, he intends to stay *a little while*) on 10 July 1826. In it he continues to complain of the influence of what he terms *the torpidity of the times from the recent confusion of the banks* on his plans to recruit subscribers, and the delays of printers. He returns Churchyard's WORTHINES OF WALES and asks permission to retain for further transcribing *the long address on Chivalry's having originated in Wales* that Thomas Price (Carnhuanawc) had given at the Brecon eisteddfod. He asks Rees to help deliver numbers (of the BALNEA) to subscribers and writes of his reluctance to incur the additional expense of binding up numbers into a complete 'part'. His financial position was, as usual, precarious.

Almost two years passed before he wrote again, on 1 July 1828, from Aberystwyth. In Pigot & Co's SOUTH WALES DIRECTORY for that year Naomi Prichard is listed as a 'straw hat maker' with premises in Great Dark-Gate Street, where John Cox, Prichard's printer in the town, also had his business. After apologizing at length for being a poor correspondent, he describes his situation:

The bad sale, or rather the failure of the 'Balnea' brought me into real pecuniary difficulties & it was long before I could make up my mind, and afterwards avow my determination, to discontinue it; and I could not write to you without stating as much. Last winter was the saddest of my life – long continued illness brought me almost to the verge of the grave . . . I have now two works in the press, 'Twm Shon Catti', & the 'Cambrian Wreath'. The latter is formed of the collection principally made at your house, & I have no doubt it will sell well. Twm Shon Catti is formed into a petite historical novel, interspersed with poems, & I was fortunate enough to collect more anecdotes respecting that worthy while travelling for Subscribers in the course of last summer. It is my intention to collect as much additional matter as I can to form another volume similar to & on the same plan as the 'Cambrian Wreath', under the title of the 'Cambrian Garland' . . .

By 26 September 1828 he is able to report that both the books have been out about ten days:

I have been very assiduous in serving the Strangers [that is, the tourists still at Aberystwyth for what remained of the 'season'] *and Subscribers here. I find that both Twm and the Wreath go off very well. A letter has just arrived from Brecon stating that a copy has reached that town & people were daily enquiring for the arrival of Twm; consequently I am just setting out for Brecon . . . I shall take the earliest opportunity of forwarding copies to your brother at Llandovery, and one of each to you at Cascob . . . I should feel obliged by your not*

*showing your copies, when you receive them, at Carmarthen, as
I have some reason for being afraid of having them pirated, to
steal a march on me, as I cannot yet get there to serve my
subscribers . . . I have great hopes of being put a little to right
with these two works. Twm Shon Catti, I conceived, is not the
sort of work in which I could express my obligations to you with
propriety in the preface, and unluckily I was confined in the
preface to the Wreath to two pages, which deprived me of the
pleasure there, but I hope in a future undertaking to have that
satisfaction . . .*

A further twenty-six years were to pass before
Prichard found the appropriate opportunity to
declare his gratitude to Rees publicly. This did not
deter his benefactor, who continued to extend to him
the hospitality of Cascob and the resources of its
library with undiminished generosity.

From the sparse evidence that has come down to us
it is difficult to conclude what sort of man Prichard
was, except that for a long time, and with very
modest success, he continued to struggle against
adversity. But if there is some sign that he had a
certain charm and could convey a sense of worth, or
at least impress with his endeavour, it is in the long
preservation of the friendship between him and
William Jenkins Rees. It says much for Rees, who
was by common consent an estimable gentleman.
Even so, one might reasonably wonder why this
relationship persisted. The good rector was at the
hub of eisteddfodic affairs and a dense network of
connections with Welsh societies and fellow clerics;
his correspondence fills many volumes. Prichard
was certainly the strangest of his great circle of
acquaintance and probably the most importunate,
but he was never turned away. More than a

Samaritan generosity of spirit would seem necessary to account for this. In 1826, Rees completed a substantial 'Pedigree and Family Connections', preserved in Cardiff Library. It shows that he too had links, distant but distinct, with the Jeffreys of Bailie Cwmdwr in the parish of Llywel. Furthermore, he, like the Revd Jeffery Llewelyn of Llywel, was a wealthy Anglican clergyman. Doubtless he had been told the whole of Prichard's story, and it would not be surprising if consistent support for the writer was prompted as much by a sense of personal responsibility for his misfortune, as by regard for his literary skills. A further indication of their closeness is communicated by the following from Prichard's letter of 26 September:

I had scarcely named to my wife your kind intention of favoring [sic] me with a copy of your Portrait before a place and a frame was assigned to it, over the mantlepiece, between her portrait and mine . . .

TWM SHÔN CATTI and THE CAMBRIAN WREATH brought some material comfort to Prichard, but his existence was ever hand-to-mouth. The former certainly attracted an unexpected level of attention. It was discussed in letters exchanged by members of that wide circle of Anglican clerics who were largely responsible for generating interest in antiquarian and literary affairs in Wales. Henry Davies, a correspondent of William Jenkins Rees writing from Cheltenham, expressed his disappointment with TWM SHÔN CATTI:

many of its anecdotes are as familiar to me as household words eg that of the Schoolmaster and the Grapes . . . I could notice several others and give them their right places. I like the

Cambrian Wreath much better. The getting up of both books will however do our Country credit which is saying a great deal.

Indeed, the book received serious consideration from some of the noted Welsh critics of the day, as Prichard himself remarked in his preface to the second edition. Dr Owen Pughe (Idrison), commenting on the book in a new journal, the CAMBRIAN QUARTERLY, complained that Twm was not accorded the honours due to his prototype, Thomas Jones. David Owen (Brutus – at this time coincidentally living at Llywel) was critical of the book for making a hero of a reprobate. Thomas Beynon, the archdeacon of Cardigan, justly venerated for the support he gave to Welsh literature, and a close friend of the rector of Cascob, praised the book as the *first Welsh novel* and offered a prize for the best translation of it into Welsh. That it was pirated as Prichard feared and that a dozen editions of TWM SHÔN CATTI, in English and Welsh, appeared between 1828 and 1904 (not to mention the adaptations that have been published since) is testimony to its enduring appeal. For Prichard, however, the benefits of its popularity were short-lived.

Some eighteen months passed before his next letter to Rees, again from Aberystwyth, on 1 March 1830. It begins with a St David's Day greeting, and a reference to the *horrible, heavy, long winter* that has oppressed him. Some literary small talk follows, about contributions intended for the *New Cambrian Quarterly* that he misdirected and were returned to him with postage to pay, about some interesting books he has acquired that Rees may wish to add to his library at Cascob, and about additions to another collection like THE CAMBRIAN WREATH (*there I shall*

*again become deeply indebted for your assistance – but I
dread publishing in these inauspicious times).* The main
purpose of the letter becomes clear in the final
paragraph:

> *I am at the moment in a pecuniary dilemma – no uncommon
> case with me – the house which I occupy has been a disputed
> property but now the affair is decided, and the triumphant party
> has suddenly come upon me with a demand for instant payment
> of rent for which unluckily I am not prepared, not anticipating
> such a claim till May at least. Thus circumstanced, I am at my
> wits' end to hunt for cash to save my few things (principally
> books) from being seized upon. I trust you will see the extreme
> urgency of the case, and excuse me when I ask whether you have
> been enabled to dispose of those books of mine which you were so
> good as to take from Carmarthen. If you have not, will you
> pardon me when I solicit the performance of a kind act – namely
> that you would advance me £2, the price of those ten copies? –
> The timely receipt of that small sum would at this moment save
> me from incalculable inconvenience. With strong hopes in your
> kindness, I hastily conclude, trusting to hear from you by
> return of post.*

As was customary he added a postscript: *My wife &
two little girls are well – Mrs P desires her best compts.*
So much for his *great hopes of being put a little to right*
with TWM SHÔN CATTI and THE CAMBRIAN WREATH.

Prichard's case was by no means unusual: im-
poverishment and debt were common in artistic
circles more illustrious than those in which he
moved. In A SULTRY MONTH (1965), a close examination of London literary life in June 1846, Alethea
Hayter recounts how the artist Benjamin Robert
Haydon, *a temperate domesticated man . . . energetic and
hard-working*, smuggled pictures and trunks
containing his papers and journals from his own

home to that of the poet Elizabeth Barrett to prevent them being seized by creditors. He had been arrested for debt seven times in the previous twenty-five years and imprisoned for debt on four occasions. 'Getting and spending' may have been viewed with melancholy scorn by Wordsworth, but, as Micawber dismally calculated, woe betide those whose expenditure exceeded their income.

In the last letter in the collection, from *Dolgelly 16th March 1830*, Prichard thanks Rees for his prompt response:

the timely receipt of your agreeable letter relieved us from considerable embarrassment. You have in this instance truly verified the proverb – 'a friend in need, is a friend indeed.' I find the bad times are as well known in North Wales as the South, at least as far as I have yet gone, where indeed the sale of my books has done but little more than pay my expenses. After my return to Aberystwyth I intend to do myself the pleasure of giving you a call at Cascob, where I should have been long ago but that I fear to involve myself further by publishing while the times are so strikingly discouraging as at present . . . I quit Dolgelly tomorrow, with rather gloomy anticipations, for I have no letter of introduction to any person in the North – At any rate I shall see something of the country, and that is highly desirable in many respects. Mrs P. desires best compts. and thanks. My brace of little lapses thank God are well.

It seems likely that some time later in the same year Prichard returned with his family to Builth and settled there. His second daughter, Senena, had been born there in 1827, presumably at the address in Cross Street, and her baptism registered at St Mary's, the parish church: *Dec. 17th Senena Daughter of Thomas and Naomi Prichard Builth Author of Welsh Minstrelsy*. Another impending birth may have precipitated the return, for a third daughter was registered on 30 December 1830: *Mevanwy Daughter of Thos. Ll. and Naomi Prichard Builth Author of Welsh Minstrelsy*. For reasons beyond guessing, this child was re-registered with an altered name on 30 October 1834, the entry on this occasion incorporating changes to the father's name and status: *Methvanwy daughter of Llewelyn and Naomi Prichard Bookseller*. Yet another daughter, Ellen, was born in March 1836, and again her parents, Llewelyn and Naomi, were identified as booksellers.

As we have seen, Prichard published a revised and much enlarged second edition of TWM SHÔN CATTY, the preface concluding, *Builth, Breconshire, August 1839*. The previous April he had signed an agreement with Josiah Thomas Jones, the printer, of Cowbridge for the production of a thousand copies. Curiously, on the title page we see that it was indeed printed by J. T. Jones, 'For E. Pool'. What can this mean? Did E. Pool pay the cost of printing? Although the agreement with the printer was signed by Prichard, was 'E. Pool' then the copyright holder? In the 1841 census for High Street, Builth, we find one Edward Poole, aged 40, of independent means, lodging with Naomi Prichard, her three-month-old son and four daughters, and Anne Prichard, aged 70. In 1851, Poole, now described as a Cambridge graduate *& priest in orders not beneficed but engaged in private tuition*, lives in Broad Street next door to Prichard's family, of which Tydvil, the eldest, is by this time head and continues the trade of bookseller. The information is difficult to interpret. It seems possible, even likely, that Anne Prichard was the writer's mother, in 1841 living with Naomi to help with the baby. Poole is a well-educated lodger, and perhaps also related to the family: shortly before he died Prichard is said to have received a gift of money from a cousin who was a clergyman, and by that time Poole was vicar of Llanfihangel and Llandewig in the county of Radnor.

Llewelyn Felix, the last child of the family, was born in March 1841. As mentioned earlier, the birth certificate bears Naomi's signature and, though the occupation of the child's father is given as 'stationer', he is not present. It is not clear that Prichard had any continuing connection with the home in Builth after 1840, though he was a witness at the marriage of his daughter Senena in May 1851. We have the evidence of correspondents to 'Bye-Gones' that he was on the stage in Aberystwyth and Brecon about 1841. Naomi Prichard died of hepatitis in 1848.

According to Prichard's great-granddaughter, Mrs Myfanwy Walters, interviewed in the 1970s, Senena, Mevanwy, Ellen and Llewelyn Felix left Builth and settled in the dockland area of Cardiff, where they opened a shop. They were living together in Peel Street there at the time of the 1861 census, the three women following their mother's occupation of milliner/dressmaker, while the 20-year-old Llewelyn Felix was a bookbinder. Family tradition had it that what remained with them of Prichard's manuscripts and papers were destroyed in the course of moving house some eighty years ago. Long before that particulars of the writer's life and death had faded to a ghostly shadow.

IX

Apart from the final seven weeks or so, our knowledge of Prichard's life from 1839 onwards remains if anything vaguer than in the period before, despite the fact that the few reminiscences of him that exist (mentioned above) all refer to these years. We have the testimony of 'Ceredig Cyfeiliog' that, in addition to acting, he was for a time employed by Lady Hall at Llanover. We know too that he devoted much time and energy to historical research and the completion of a project that seems to have occupied him intermittently from the mid-1820s, when he first began accumulating historical materials in connection with the BALNEA and became engrossed in books he found in the library at Cascob. What prompted him to concentrate on the task towards the end of the 1840s (the death of his wife? the loss of his nose?) must be a matter for conjecture. He needed the support of a patron and access to books. The connection with Lady Hall at Llanover was important in both respects, but the convenient task of cataloguing the books in her library, mentioned by the 'Bye-Gones' correspondent, seems not to have lasted. Without mentioning names (Augusta Hall, by this time Lady Llanover, was still alive in 1889 when he wrote the article), Charles Wilkins describes how Prichard would declaim *against the narrow-souled inheritor of riches who wouldn't help him*:

He once told me how his downfall began. For years he was occupied with a great historical work. He had a patron who encouraged him. Life was happy. As he progressed with his work he saw fame in the distant future, and comfort and rest. But his patron, who scrupulously examined his manuscript, began to find fault. He had to choose between historic accuracy or the entire withdrawal of his patron's support. He was not required to make false statements but to slur over facts. And this he would not do, and he added, 'I was turned adrift, too poor to go on unaided, and then began my downward course.'

The likely cause of the rift was the Welsh language. As we have seen, in the 1820s, Prichard had been an enthusiastic supporter of the language. This attitude, which probably owed a good deal to the influence of the CAMBRO-BRITON, did not persist, though whether the change was gradual or brought about by a particular event it is not possible to guess. In HEROINES there is an undercurrent of controversy, seen at the outset in the preface, which is largely a critique of those the writer termed *the Fanatics of Welsh Nationality*. The views expressed in it were diametrically opposed to those of Lady Hall, who in the years 1847–9, when it seems very likely Prichard was at Llanover, was embroiled in the organization of protest against the report of the government's commissioners into the state of education in Wales, the *treachery of the Blue Books*. Her unpublished letters of this period to William Rees, printer, of Llandovery (nephew of William Jenkins Rees) about ARTEGALL, the anonymous response to the commissioners' report, which she may well have stimulated and certainly saw through to publication, reveal a woman exacting in her demands, who brooked no opposition and was quick to express disappointment and anger at the perceived failings of others. Since both she and Prichard were blunt, even vehement, in writing, and probably no less so in their speech, it is easy to see why they fell out.

HEROINES is vitriolically dedicated *To the Virtuous Votaries of True Womanhood . . . As Contra-Distinguished From The Fantastic Fooleries And Artificial Characteristics of Fine Ladyism In The Middle Walks Of Life*, and the single direct reference to Lady Hall is a dry acknowledgement at the end of the preface that her interest obtained for him admission to the library of the British Museum. Warmer thanks are reserved for the rector of Cascob:

In especial terms . . . I express my gratitude to the Rev. William Jenkins Rees . . . not only for the personal aid which he rendered me in transcribing from the valuable books in his library, and his Manuscript History of Radnorshire, but at an unfortunate period in my life, for the hospitality of his house for many weeks while so employed, during the inclemency of a severe winter.

The preface also gives credit (at last) to John Humffreys Parry for his CAMBRIAN PLUTARCH (1824), as the inspiration of a work on Welsh history presented (in Parry's words) *in a form more qualified to allure the general reader; namely, an English costume.* Another source and influence was THE HISTORIE OF CAMBRIA (1584), that is to say, David Powel's redaction of Humffrey Llwyd's translation of the chronicle attributed to Caradog of Llancarfan. Both suggested an approach to history in 'chapters' devoted to individual figures. In the HISTORIE, they are the Welsh Princes, beginning with Cadwalader and ending, thanks to Powel's addition of the 'Princes of Wales of the English Blood', with Elizabeth I, though significantly the final page is devoted to Sir Henry Sidney, Lord President of Wales under Elizabeth, who commissioned the book. The choice of female rather than male figures for chapter headings in HEROINES is largely cosmetic, since all the sources available had considerably more to say about the latter. Surveying the whole episode, it seems reasonable to speculate that the book was conceived in a way which should allow a chapter to be devoted to Lady Hall, or at least a final tribute made to her contribution to the heritage and culture of Wales. On such a basis Prichard might have enjoyed a sinecure at Llanover and the access he needed to its library. Instead of Lady Hall, however, the reader is given 'Dolly of Pentraeth', an intrusion from Cornish history that might be thought arbitrary, were it not for its message about the death of a language, which

> cannot but come home, doubly charged with pathetic reference, to the bosom of every Welchman [sic] or Celt . . . whose language, notwithstanding every effort made or making for its support or revival, is also on the eve of extinction.

It might even have been a calculated insult to the patron who dismissed him.

HEROINES was offered to the public as a single bound volume of almost six hundred pages, priced seven shillings and sixpence, or in six numbers at one shilling each. (He had, he said, enough material in manuscript to make a second volume of similar size.) It was printed by C. T. Jefferies (that name again!) in Bristol, and following its publication, the writer, in his mid-sixties, once more took to the road. It was at this time that Charles Wilkins met him in Merthyr, when Prichard's usual practice *was to get consignments of the volume sent to him at various towns, and with these he went literally from door to door selling them.* The letter Prichard wrote from *Major Roteley's Cottage, Thomas-street, World's End, Swansea, 24th*

Nov., 1857 to an unnamed correspondent, printed in Wilkins's article, begins with the making of such an arrangement:

Herewith I enclose you a Post Office Order for £2 2s., for which I will thank you to forward me 14 copies of my Book, to be sent per Railway, addressed – To the care of Mrs. Whittington, Postmistress, Neath . . .

I am now about to travel and re-commence my Bookselling. I have lately written a long letter to Jefferies explanatory of the very long illness with which I have been afflicted, and which kept me an invalid, after being confined indoors and mostly in bed the whole of last summer, to the great detriment of my interests in the sale of my Book. But I heartily thank my gracious God my intellects were not dormant during the period of my bodily affliction, for I have done much towards future publications – especially one which will bear the title of/ Raps At The Russians . . . But I shall never publish again, except on the terms of selling the copyright to a London publisher – with the sole exception of my very fortunate book, The Adventures and Vagaries of Twm Shôn Catty, that the people seem wild about seeing in print again . . . I have delayed re-publishing it from an intention of re-writing the whole, in which, with the forenamed, I have in a great degree employed myself during the suspension of my travelling capabilities, so that in the end I think my illness will ultimately prove as productive – and probably more so, than if I had been solely employed in selling the Heroines of Welsh History – which, I regret to say, is far from meeting with similar popularity to that accorded to Twm Shôn Catty – although it deserves it far more, being Historical . . .

Wilkins's *poor, haggard man* with his wax nose and *earnest snuffle* might well have been a figure of fun to the unsympathetic. So, indeed, he was to the gangs of children who roamed the backstreets of Swansea. The next report of any sort to have survived is a long-forgotten account in the CAMBRIAN newspaper

(22 November 1861) of an old man's appalling and helpless predicament. It arises from a letter to the mayor of the town, which he in turn calls to the attention of the superintendent of police:

'Bird-in-Hand, High-street, Swansea, November 18, 1861. – Sir, – An aged and infirm old gentleman, Llewelyn Prichard, author of the "Heroines of Welsh Poetry" [sic] and other works of considerable note, dwells in the late Major Roteley's cottage, and to my great sorrow I yesterday (Sunday) morning witnessed a number of ruffians, boys and girls, residing in the neighbourhood, most ruthlessly molesting the cottage, throwing stones in showers at his door and windows, and when he came out and bade them desist, they mercilessly insulted him. The favour of your directing the Superintendent's attention to this matter, and publicly inviting the neighbours who are witnesses of such gross acts of inhumanity, to aid the police in bringing to justice these incorrigibles who so richly deserve it, will greatly oblige, yours respectfully, W. Yorath.' At a subsequent sitting of the Magistrates, Mr. Dunn said he had visited the house of Mr. Prichard in Thomas-street, and a more pitiable and distressing scene he had never witnessed. The unfortunate man was lying on his bed apparently seriously ill, and so far as could be discovered completely destitute; the single room on the ground floor which he inhabited, was as cheerless and as wretched as any Grub-street garret in the last century could possibly have been – a chaos of dirty and dusty books, pamphlets and MSS. in prose and poetry, with scarcely a vestige of furniture, and without provisions of any kind. Among the heap of papers with which the chamber was crammed, were copies of various of Mr. Prichard's published works, and a manuscript volume entitled 'Medallions of the Memorable, in a series of historic essays and sonnets.' The works in question, both published and unpublished, seem to display considerable literary merit as well as great historical research. It is a positive fact that this wretched old gentleman did not taste a mouthful of bread from Saturday morning last until Monday middle day, but subsisted upon two or three half-diseased potatoes which he managed to roast by means of a small fire made of scraps

95

of wood, &c, which he had also picked up in the streets. With an honest (though perhaps silly) pride, Mr. Prichard positively refuses an asylum in the Union, declaring that he will starve rather than being an indoor pauper. We are glad to be able to state that orders have been given to have the dwelling of this poor old gentleman thoroughly cleaned, and efforts are being made to induce the Board of Guardians to allow him weekly out-door relief. At most the sum which the Guardians can legitimately give is but a poor pittance, and we are sure that we have said enough to induce all true-hearted Welshmen to subscribe a sufficient sum in order that this poor old gentleman may pass the remainder of his days in comparative ease and comfort. Any sums forwarded to Supt. Dunn will be properly applied.

The following week (29 November) a more cheerful notice appeared:

We are sincerely glad to be able to say that the condition of this poor old gentleman has been much bettered during the past week . . . Through the kind instrumentality of Mr. Essery, surgeon of the Board of Guardians, the house has been thoroughly cleansed, the old and rickety bedstead has been destroyed and its place occupied by a new iron one, and warm and comfortable bedding has been supplied. One or two good suits of clothes have been provided, his daily wants met by voluntary contributions, and the whole external aspect of the place completely altered. Tears and prayers bespeak the old man's gratitude. The Board of Guardians have consented to allow Mr. Prichard 5s. per week as out-door relief, and contributions from various parts are rolling in rather freely. On Wednesday evening last, a committee meeting was held in the house of Mr. Wm. Morris, when arrangements were made for obtaining still larger contributions, so as to enable this much pitied old gentleman, and once able writer, to end the remainder of his days in comparative ease.

The frequently repeated assertion that Prichard died in Swansea Union Workhouse is seen to be incorrect, though he missed that fate by his own stubbornness and a hair's breadth. Nor is it strictly true that he died in poverty; the good offices of certain individuals and the publicity of his plight afforded by the CAMBRIAN saved him from that. One outcome of the 'committee meeting' may have been a scheme to provide further aid by the sale of his manuscripts (perhaps to the Wm. Morris mentioned in the newspaper report, who is probably the William Morris of Swansea listed among the publishers of HEROINES), as described in the preface to the third edition of TWM SHÔN CATTI, including the additions and alterations Prichard made to the novel while he lay ill in 1857. That he got no further with these amendments than the third chapter is an indication of the sickness and despair that afflicted his last years. And even now the days of 'comparative ease' were destined to be very few. A brief news item in the CAMBRIAN on 10 January 1862 gave a garbled account of an accident that had befallen him. The following week's issue (17 January) told the whole pathetic story:

Death of Llewelyn Prichard, The Poet

An inquest was held before C. Collins, Esq., Coroner, on Saturday evening last, at the Hop-Pole Inn, Edward-street, on the body of Mr. Llewelyn Prichard, aged 72, who died the previous day from the effects of severe burns which he had accidentally received . . . The Coroner having briefly stated the facts of the case the Jury proceeded to view the body, which was lying in his house at World's End. Upon the re-assembling of the jury, the following evidence was given:-

Esther Bird, upon being sworn, said: I have been in attendance upon the deceased for the past two months, having been employed to do so by the parish authorities. He lived alone in a house in Thomas-street, Edward-street. He occupied the room where the body now lies. About half past 9 on Thursday morning last, I went to the deceased's room as usual to do what was necessary. I opened the shutters and pushed the door open and went into his room. He was then sitting on the side of the bed with his drawers and stockings on only. On going in I said, 'Oh, my God, what is the matter?' He said, 'Oh! the boys – the boys.' I saw from the state of his clothes that he had been burnt. They were nearly burnt to pieces. Some were lying on the bed and some on the ground. The deceased was dreadfully burnt on the arm and back and neck. I observed that the deceased had thrown water over himself. He mostly remained up all night. I saw the deceased about 9 o'clock the night previous. He was then very comfortable with a good fire. The deceased was unconscious and could not give me any account of what had happened, he said his left arm was asleep. I went and called a neighbour and then went for Mr. Essery, surgeon, and when I came back I found him on the ground with the neighbours around him. Mr. Essery attended him immediately. The round table which he used was thrown down against the fire. I made the bed the previous night before I left him, and on going in in the morning it did not appear as though it had been slept in. It did not appear to me as though he had been drinking. He used to be out all hours of the night. I attended the deceased until he died, which was about six o'clock this morning. The deceased recovered his senses and talked more rationally yesterday evening. He did not express any wish to see anybody. He had plenty of everything. On Wednesday last the deceased told me he had received £5 from a cousin of his who is a clergyman. On Thursday morning last the deceased showed me four sovereigns in gold, and I believe 15s. 6d. in silver. There was some spirits (rum) in a bottle. I believe Mr. George redeemed some things with part of the money. The deceased did not like the idea of receiving parish relief and it was paid through other person's hands.

William Peters said: I knew the deceased Llewelyn Prichard. I saw him between 11 and 12 o'clock on Wednesday night in Thomas-street going in the direction of the house in which he lived. I did not speak to him. I do not know where he had been. I told Mr. Dunn that I had seen the deceased at the time stated. I told Mr. Dunn that I believed the deceased had had a little drop too much. I believe he had been drinking a little, I saw the *deceased with a bottle before that evening. He walked as steadily as usual. I think the deceased came from the Gardener's Arms.*

Ann Norman said: I knew the deceased. I saw him at the Gardener's Arms at about nine o'clock on Wednesday night. I believe he had a noggin of rum with me. I served him. He did not sit down. He did not appear to be at all under the influence of liquor. He often opened the door to see what time it was.

Thomas Aubrey Essery, Surgeon, deposed: A little after ten o'clock on Thursday morning last I was called to see the deceased. I found him severely burnt over the chest, the arms and the back; there was a slight burn on the face. He had been supplied with remedies from my surgery before I arrived. He was in a very low state. I continued to attend him until he died. He continued in a low state from the shock to the system and the burns. I saw him yesterday. The effects of the burns and the shock to the constitution were the cause of death. I have been in attendance on the deceased occasionally for about two months. He did not appear in want of anything.

The jury, without hesitation, returned a verdict of 'Accidental Death.'

Mr. Yorath made a few observations with the view of shewing that the deceased had been properly cared for, and the private subscriptions which had poured in from all quarters were quite sufficient to keep him in comfort and to provide him with every necessary. It was also stated that there were quite sufficient funds in hand to bury the deceased in a respectable and decent manner.

His sudden rediscovery in destitution, the raising of a subscription on his behalf that allowed him to be set up in reasonable comfort, and his death by accident might be thought events unusual enough to have fixed at least Prichard's final days in popular memory. Within twenty years of the inquest, however, estimates of the date of his death were inaccurate by as much as thirteen years. Even his burial place was lost: the DICTIONARY OF NATIONAL BIOGRAPHY quotes CYFAILL YR AELWYD, 1887, to the effect that he was interred in Tabernacle graveyard in Swansea, but that was not so. He has a plot in Danygraig Cemetery, on a hill overlooking the town and the bay.

Prichard has a claim to being the first conscious, even determined, Anglo-Welsh writer. His final words to the reading public have been echoed by Welsh writers in English down to the present. In his preface to HEROINES OF WELSH HISTORY he writes of the

crying vice of our Welshland portion of Britain, a most apathetic and discreditable indifference – not only to literature in general, and their own country's history in particular – but to everything except the accumulation of property . . . When once this head of mine, such as it is, is laid low (and the period is not remote), though many more gifted may arise, but you will not readily meet another so patient under your niggardly patronage – so content to walk the same path through regions so unpromising of either laurels or profit; – and the more intelligent may yet have to regret the encouragement withheld, or niggardly bestowed, from finishing a Work that their children may prize more than their dull apathetic parents.

Bibliography

Poetry

MY LOWLY LOVE AND OTHER PETITE POEMS, CHIEFLY ON WELSH SUBJECTS, Worthing (printed by William Phillips), 1822.

MARIETTE MOULINE, THE DEATH OF GLYNDOWER, AND OTHER POEMS, PARTLY ON WELSH SUBJECTS, London (printed by W. Hersee), 1823.

WELSH MINSTRELSY: CONTAINING THE LAND BENEATH THE SEA; OR, CANTREV Y GWAELOD, A POEM IN THREE CANTOS; WITH VARIOUS OTHER POEMS, London, John and H. L. Hunt (printed by John Cox, Aberystwyth), 1824.

ABERYSTWITH IN MINIATURE, IN VARIOUS POEMS, Carmarthen (printed by Jonathan Harris), 1824.

THE CAMBRIAN WREATH; A SELECTION OF ENGLISH POEMS ON WELSH SUBJECTS, ORIGINAL AND TRANSLATED FROM THE CAMBRO-BRITISH, HISTORIC AND LEGENDARY, INCLUDING WELSH MELODIES: BY VARIOUS AUTHORS OF CELEBRITY, LIVING AND DEPARTED, Aberystwyth (printed by John Cox), 1828.

Prose

THE NEW ABERYSTWYTH GUIDE TO THE WATERS, BATHING HOUSES, PUBLIC WALKS, AND AMUSEMENTS;

INCLUDING HISTORICAL NOTICES AND GENERAL INFORMATION ETC., Aberystwyth (printed by John Cox for Lewis Jones), 1824.

THE CAMBRIAN BALNEA: OR GUIDE TO THE WATERING PLACES OF WALES, MARINE AND INLAND (Part I: THE LLANDRINDOD GUIDE), London, John and H. L. Hunt (printed by Price, Printer, Hay), 1825.

THE ADVENTURES AND VAGARIES OF TWM SHÔN CATTI; DESCRIPTIVE OF LIFE IN WALES: INTERSPERSED WITH POEMS, Aberystwyth (printed by John Cox), 1828.

THE ADVENTURES AND VAGARIES OF TWM SHÔN CATTY ALIAS THOMAS JONES, ESQ., OF TREGARON, A WILD WAG OF WALES, Second edition, Cowbridge (printed for E. Pool by J. T. Jones), 1839.

HEROINES OF WELSH HISTORY: COMPRISING MEMOIRS AND BIOGRAPHICAL NOTICES OF THE CELEBRATED WOMEN OF WALES, ESPECIALLY THE EMINENT FOR TALENT, THE EXEMPLARY IN CONDUCT, THE ECCENTRIC IN CHARACTER, AND THE CURIOUS BY POSITION, OR OTHERWISE, London, W. & F. G. Cash; Bristol, C. T. Jefferies; Swansea, William Morris, 1854.

THE ADVENTURES AND VAGARIES OF TWM SHÔN CATTI ALIAS THOMAS JONES, ESQ., OF TREGARON, A WILD WAG OF WALES, Third edition, Now First Printed From MSS Left By The Author, Llanidloes, John Pryse, 1873.

Critical Commentary

Gerald Morgan, 'The First Anglo-Welsh Novel', THE ANGLO-WELSH REVIEW, Vol. 17, No. 39, 1968.

Sam Adams, 'Thomas Jeffery Llewelyn Prichard',
THE ANGLO-WELSH REVIEW, Vol. 24, No. 52, 1974.

Sam Adams, 'Thomas Jeffery Llewelyn Prichard',
BRYCHEINIOG, Vol. XXI, 1985.

Acknowledgements

It was Roland Mathias who first suggested I interest myself in T. J. Llewelyn Prichard, guided my early attempts to get to grips with a decidedly slippery customer, and was good enough to print the outcome in THE ANGLO-WELSH REVIEW. In this, as in so many other things, I owe a great deal to the stimulus of his curiosity about all aspects of literature, and his constant encouragement. I am deeply indebted also to Mrs Patricia Curtis, who, attracted by the oddness and mystery of Prichard, pursued her own researches into the many unknown corners of his life. She not only discovered a good deal, but generously shared her discoveries with me and so kept my interest alive. Her reward was to find and lay flowers on Prichard's grave at Danygraig Cemetery, overlooking Swansea Bay, while a rainbow arched overhead.

I am very grateful to a number of individuals, including Mary Ellis, Revd Nigel Hall (vicar of St Mary's, Builth Wells), Sr Bonaventure Kelleher (the Ursuline Convent, Brecon), Gerald Morgan, R. C. B. Oliver (The Radnorshire Society), E. G. Parry (Christ College, Brecon), Gwynedd Pierce ('Ditectif Geiriau'), Helen Gichard and Peter Powell of the Brecknock Society and Museum Friends, and Thomas Howell Watkins and Revd and Mrs Warrington of Llywel, who all took pains to reply to my enquiries, even if they were unable to offer substantial help; and to staff of the following institutions: the libraries at Swansea, Brecon, Brighton and Worthing, Lambeth Palace Library, the Study Room of the National Museum of the Performing Arts, Covent Garden, the Meteorological Office Archives at Bracknell, the Powys County Archive Office, Llandrindod Wells, almost all of whom helped to add something to the stock of circumstantial evidence to speculate upon, and especially the National Library of Wales and Cardiff Central Library, where significant new materials towards the life and work of Prichard were waiting to be found.

The Author

Sam Adams is a native of Gilfach Goch in Glamorgan. He obtained an honours degree and an MA in English from the University College of Wales, Aberystwyth. He taught in a comprehensive school in Bristol and at Caerleon College of Education before joining Her Majesty's Inspectorate of Schools. He has now retired and lives in Caerleon.

He is a former editor of the magazine POETRY WALES, and a former chairman of the English-language section of Yr Academi Gymreig.

With Roland Mathias, he co-edited THE SHINING PYRAMID AND OTHER STORIES BY WELSH AUTHORS (Gomer, 1970), and was editor of TEN ANGLO-WELSH POETS (Carcanet, 1974). He is the author of the volumes on GERAINT GOODWIN and ROLAND MATHIAS for the Writers of Wales Series (UWP, 1975 and 1995). His second book of poems, JOURNEYING (Gomer), was published in 1994.

Designed by Jeff Clements
Typesetting at the University of Wales Press in
11pt Palatino and printed in Great Britain by
Dinefwr Press, Llandybïe, 2000

British Library Cataloguing in Publication Data.
A catalogue record for this book is available from the
British Library.

ISBN 0-7083-1645-X

The Publishers wish to acknowledge the financial
assistance of the Arts Council of Wales towards the cost
of producing this volume.